I0060630

THE *first home* BUYERS GUIDE

Believing in everyone's ability to buy a home

PETER MASTROIANNI

Copyright ©2015 Peter Mastroianni

All rights reserved. No part of this book may be reproduced or transmitted in any form or by any means, electronic or mechanical, including photocopying, recording, or by any information storage and retrieval system, without written permission from the author. Any unauthorised use, sharing, reproduction, or distribution is prohibited.

Disclaimer:
This eBook does not necessarily reflect the opinion of the publisher. It is intended to provide general news and information only. It does not take into account your personal objectives, financial situation or needs.

While every care has been taken to ensure accurate information is presented, neither the publishers, author nor their employees, can be held liable for inaccuracies, errors or omission.

Readers are advised to contact their financial adviser, broker or accountant before making any investment decisions and should not rely on this eBook as a substitute for professional advice. This information is to be used as a guide only and is subject to change at any time.

Typeset & formatting by: Access Ideas, access.ideas@yahoo.com

Contents

INTRODUCTION

Owning your first home is a great thing. It's the Australian dream, right? It's an investment in your future. A place to call "your own", a comfortable place to sleep and brings the potential to create a platform for something even greater.

Our feelings towards our homes can sometimes be irrational due to our emotional attachment to them. They become a haven enabling us to raise a family, to entertain, relax and provide a worthwhile long-term investment. They can indicate to the world that you are doing well for yourself therefore can become a marker of status and success.

So will your new home be a happy playground or a dead weight? It's really just a matter of perception.

What truly matters is how you feel about your own decision. A big debt at any age can be crippling or incredibly motivating depending upon your mind-set. If your innermost desire is to buy and you are ready to embrace some creative tension in your life, then just accept that you are welcoming fear into your life and it is time to get comfortable with it. Fear should be viewed as a friend to nurture and respect; it goes hand in hand with buying a home.

The creative tension is the process of change. Lifestyle and habits will likely require a significant shift. Worry, stress, bills and repayments will now become annoying friends that you wish would just contact you less. But it's all part of the process. Admittedly, when I first bought a house I wasn't ready. Eighteen years old, I knew everything and had experienced nothing. I enjoyed my life, the freedom and owning a house. The parties were regular, noise was probably a constant, and for a period of time I considered myself to be a suburban King - the King of 700 square metres in the southern suburbs of Brisbane that is, and I loved it.

Reflecting on this now, I completely realise that I was an asshole. But what 18-year-old isn't?

It was a fantastic experience, an amazing opportunity and it's allowed me to be extremely fortunate over the following years. $143,500 for a four-bedroom house within 8km of the Brisbane CBD. Opportunities like that are very few and far between. I was able to sell that property in a little over 12 months for a significant profit. This was less about smarts and more about luck, that little thing known as "being in the right place at the right time." Thankfully, it was a fantastic personal learning experience and an eye-opener to how the property market works, in its most basic form. It's certainly helped me make better-informed decisions for numerous subsequent property transactions.

This initial transaction provided me with confidence for the future because of the knowledge I gained about buying and selling real estate. My initial foray into the real estate market provided me with peace of mind. Making more informed decisions about future purchases became pivotal because excitement quickly wanes, next to the stress that is associated with on-going bills and repayments.

Therefore the intention of this book is to provide guidance on your journey to buying a home, easing the route to success. The book is structured in a way to address the major questions you will have as you go through the steps of purchasing your first home. A "101" with just enough sizzle to make you a little dangerous in a competitive market.

The following pages will guide you through:

1. What does a first home look like.
   Types, characteristics and pros & cons of the options available.

2. Saving. How to kill debt and start growing a nest egg.
   Possessing the desire and creating the ability to contribute to a debt minimisation and saving strategy.

3. Securing finance.
   Qualifying your borrowing ability and finalising your loan.

4. Sourcing and buying property.
   Research methods and guiding you through the purchasing process.

5. Sorting out the rules of engagement and getting the "admin" right.
   Offer, negotiation, purchase and settlement.

6. Miscellaneous items and other considerations
   Preparing your house and shedding light on your alternative options.

Having the information can help your "process awareness", hence why this book provides the fundamentals, hints/ tips, FAQs, explanations of terms and so much more.

From where you sit now, your dream is really not that far away. It is a great feeling but it is a change from your norm. It will likely require a change in spending habits, require your personal time to research, manage, and keep up with the latest data but once you're in, that hard work won't really seem to matter. Be real with your expectations, be patient and don't get caught up in market hype. And most importantly be proud of your achievement along with what you have created as that "creative tension" won't seem so tense in hindsight.

Being informed through each step is the key to success. www.thebuyersguide.com.au is here to inform and provide the necessary information to help smooth the journey forward. So check the website, read the book, post your own feedback, request additional support and reach out to partner suppliers to ensure you get the necessary help to be in your own place sooner.

WHAT DOES A FIRST HOME LOOK LIKE

The word 'home' is often discussed, mentioned, shared in stories or songs and we usually have a deep psychological attachment to them. I believe this is initiated by the resilience and perseverance shown to actually get one. There is no doubt that the journey that you embark upon will be difficult at times, but coming through that, overcoming the stress of the move, unpacking, having the house styled to your liking means that it's ready for 'nesting'. After all, home is where the heart is...

CONSIDERATIONS PRIOR TO BUYING – WHAT DO BUYERS LOOK FOR

Home ownership is a fine choice to make but is one that shouldn't be taken lightly. The process can be long, difficult, stressful and expensive. So are you truly ready? Consider the factors below, be truthful and then make a decision and one that is right for YOU.

Buy because:

1. It truly makes sense financially and you are ready
2. It's better for your housing dollar than the other options available to you
3. It's what you want. It's what you can handle and it's not because of what others want
4. It is fit for your life purposes now.

What you shouldn't do is:

1. Buy because you've been told that's what you're supposed to do
2. Buy because Uncle Ted told you it's a good investment for your future
3. Buy because of the hypothetical future, with lots of kids, horses and room to expand
4. And definitely don't buy to 'keep up'.

Buying won't change who you are. No matter what idealised thoughts you have. Buy because it's actually what you want in your life right now. Forget the hype, pressure and stress and take the time to make the right decision on the right place for you.

Lifestyle, personal tastes, working and family circumstances will influence your buying choice. Being a first home buyer the top considerations for most will be:

1. Affordability
2. Size and space for living, sleeping and parking
3. Location and proximity to work, family, transport and infrastructure
4. Capital growth.

As you will note, capital growth was the last consideration. Remember, buying a home is not always about making money. As you can see, there are lots of considerations and just as many options. Everyone is different, looking at different things, all at different times. Weirdly, this all takes place in the same market vortex - it's a complete paradox when you think about it. Therefore, one could only conclude that everyone's dream is out there influenced by the decisions you make along the way.

Difference between buyers and sellers' markets and their characteristics.

When is it best to buy? This is a classic question and like all markets the property market fluctuates between the highs and lows with recovery periods in between. Think of it like the weather seasons:

- Winter; cold with a gloomy outlook
- Spring; things are starting to look brighter with some signs of life
- Summer; she's hot and everyone wants to be out there and amongst it
- Autumn; the sting is taken out of the heat and things are cooling down but action is still taking place.

The seasons are much like the property cycle in going from boom to slowing down to slump to recovery. This cycle on average takes approximately seven or so years. There are opportunities in all markets and variable characteristics that will favour one person's preferences to another. Economic, social and political factors will influence the 'weather conditions' but in most cases the property cycle will either favour the sellers or the buyers.

First home buyers may just get an upper hand in a buyer's market as conditions will favour an increase in property stock volumes and flat/ suppressed prices. These factors may indicate wider problems from a market perspective (relating to economic, social and political related aspects) but it still might be a worthwhile time to take stock and put an acid test on the market to find your ideal home.

The market conditions to look out for include:

1. Increased property sales available – lots of stock is available on the market
2. Lower listing sale prices
3. Price averages and growth percentage margins are down in consecutive quarters.
4. More advertising, and real estate agents are "chummier" and proactive in their pursuit of you as a buyer.

These conditions could be localised or have a broader market undertone. Determining these factors through some simple research at the beginning of your journey will put you at a distinct advantage, particularly in a buyer's market. And the reverse conditions will be in place during a seller's market.

Depending on your motivations, a good time to buy can realistically be in any "weather condition" but be mindful of making these mistakes:

1. Not doing enough research or lacking a true understanding of what you are entering into.

2. Buying on emotion. If you miss out on your "dream house", don't worry there are plenty of other fish in the sea.

3. Relying on non-experts. Don't skimp on good advice particularly on legal matters. Contracts are king and broaden your property conversation circles to others outside friends and family at weekend BBQs.

4. Overextending financially. Whilst you think you can afford that place priced at an extra $20k, things can quickly change. Interest rates rise, redundancies can be commonplace, bills will continue to come in and kids get hungry. And some or more of these can happen at the same time.

5. Analysis paralysis. Over-thinking everything and not making a decision can sometimes be the worst thing.

Renting versus Buying

Drum roll please ... and queue the commentators but both are fine choices. Depending on where you would like to live and what lifestyle benefits and plans you have for the foreseeable future, either circumstance could be appropriate. Rent money is dead money. Interest repayments can also be viewed as dead money.

If you move around a lot or have particular lifestyle choices, renting can be the right option for you.

The big difference is that buying a home is a fantastic personal achievement and one that is loaded with emotion. A home becomes a haven to raise a family, an environment to create as your own and ultimately one you'll eventually own outright.

Timing and circumstances are the true factors that will determine whether buying or renting is the right choice for you. Timing will be dictated by personal choices, market influences and circumstances again will fluctuate from the ups and downs of your own life and those other differentiators of the market.

Time is without a doubt the biggest influencer in deciding a winner between buying and renting as an option. Time definitely favours buying for two main reasons:

Firstly, after 25 years (or more or less) of consistently contributing to the original mortgage value through repayments you will own that property outright. Those repayments can now be used for lifestyle choices or a nice addition to your retirement saving plan. Now if you rent for the next 25 years unfortunately you won't own the property and you will have the ongoing weekly cost that you need to maintain.

Secondly, time allows the magic of compound interest to take effect. Historically, Australian house prices have almost doubled every ten years. Now this is not guaranteed as some properties will underperform but this is consistent average return equates to 7%. For example, if you buy a $450k home today, in 10 years, the value could look something like this:

1. $450,000 × 7% = $31,500
2. $481,500 × 7% = $33,705
3. $515,205 × 7% = $36,064
4. $551,269 × 7% = $38,589
5. $589,858 × 7% = $41,290
6. $631,148 × 7% = $44,180
7. $675,328 × 7% = $47,273
8. $722,600 × 7% = $50,582
9. $773,182 × 7% = $54,122
10. $827,304 × 7% = $57,911
11. $885,215

Hypothetically, in 10 years, you have almost literally doubled the value of your home through capital growth. This is obviously going to fluctuate but even if you halved the expected annual growth over 10 years serious, value will have accumulated. However, be very mindful that capital growth cannot be guaranteed. Depending on the economic factors and the actual property you own, the percentage return could vary considerably year-on-year.

Therefore, do the math and run some of your own hypothetical scenarios. Because in 25 years, you could potentially own the home outright and have achieved a significant increase in the actually value of your home.

Time = advantage buying!

Barriers of entry

In this lucky country of ours we experience a particularly high standard of living. The attraction of this lifestyle also equates to a high cost of living and housing prices. Contributing factors to high house prices include:

- There is a housing shortage and our population is growing.
- We have a safe and robust economy where profits can be made.
- Banking institutions have strict lending criteria.

- Interest rates are low - money is cheap.
- Baby boomers and investors are cashed-up and are shopping for investment properties or unlocking their superannuation through their self-managed funds.
- Our economy, weather and way of life appeals to foreign investors.

These conditions are unlikely to change quickly and most commentators agree that things are currently moving at a rather sedate pace. Reasons include the increase in building approvals, wage growth that has plateaued, and interest rates will not stay at historically low levels forever. Although, the longer you wait as a first home buyer the higher the likelihood of price rises. Over the long-term, prices tend to be higher in a slump compared to the previous slump. As we discussed, the 'weather seasons' go from hot to cold but, averaged out, prices are generally trending up.

The major hurdles faced as a first home buyer are:

1. Affordability

2. Saving for an initial deposit (refer to pp. 43 for help)

3. Purchasing costs namely Stamp Duty (refer to pp. 91)

4. Where to actually buy? (Refer to
   www.thebuyersguide.com.au for recent
   listings).

Money, money, money ... it appears like it is an
uphill battle. Saving for a deposit can be a real
slog and the costs associated with purchasing
can at times be equal to the deposit saved.
Presently, there is a little bit of help available
through the First Home Buyers Grant (refer to
pp. 94) and Stamp Duty Concessions (refer to pp.
94).

The Buyers Guide is a free resource that is here
to help and will be beneficial for First Home
Buyers. Like the thought contributors of
Independent Senator Nick Xenophon and
Treasurer Joe Hockey who have their finger on
the pulse and proposed the idea of accessing
your superannuation to help secure your first
home. Great idea! The pros and cons can be
argued by others but it is that kind of thought (at
a government level) that is required, in order for
Australians to get into their first homes sooner.
Realistically, any fundamental changes that take
place through concessions particularly by the
government will take a long time to come into
effect. So what are currently some options to
consider in order to get into your own home
sooner?

1. Don't go it alone. Buy with a friend, family
   member or the special someone (refer to
   pp. 160).

2. Use a Guarantor on your home loan (refer to pp. 88).

3. 'Flex' on some of your needs and wants. The biggest barrier might be your own expectations.

4. Buy an investment property instead (refer to pp. 156).

Accountability and responsibility are required as relying on things to change for your own benefit is not a great option. Take things in your stride, educate yourself on the process and in time it will happen. View any help received as just an added bonus. As difficult as it may seem, when you start focusing your attention on the end goal, you'll surprise yourself with what can happen.

What does a first home look like?

Depending on your budget, taste, circumstances, needs, wants and time-frame requirements will determine what your home actually looks like.

As everyone is an individual the characteristics of your first purchase could vary wildly from one person to the next. To personalise it for you, let's commence with a visualisation exercise. The power of imagination is a beautiful life tool:

Alice laughed: "there's no use trying," she said; "one can't believe impossible things."

"I daresay you haven't had much practice," said the Queen.

"When I was younger, I always did it for half an hour a day.

Why sometimes I've believed as many as six impossible things before breakfast."

.... Alice in Wonderland – Lewis Carroll; 1865

"All that we are is a result of what we have thought."

.... Buddha

So taking inspiration from Alice in Wonderland and Buddha, I want you to start by closing your eyes and take three deep breaths. Now let me ask you this - if I could wave my magical wand and create the ideal first home what would it look like? Now write it down:

Re-read what you have written and now close your eyes again and picture what it looks like. What is the colour scheme? Where is natural light coming in? What does "vegging out" on the couch look like? It is very important to visualise these aspects and others because I want that image to burn into your imagination. Keeping this little dream safely tucked away in your inner sanctum is worthwhile as your gut will instinctively shout out when you've found the right place.

I'm a bricks and mortar type of guy. It's probably the Italian coming out in me and my love affair with concrete. Now this may not be best suited to everyone, and others' preferences may not sit well with me either. Importantly, no matter what your preferences are, consideration should be given to nearby amenities as they will have a big influence on your ultimate decision, potential growth and general feel for the place. Therefore, consider:

- Transport – bus, ferry, train, taxi, tram, highway links, and express tunnels etc. Good transport links can have a significant impact on pricing and future growth.

- Shops/urban community areas – you may not have much money to splash around but some window-shopping can be a good time-killer. Plus, who wants to drive 30 minutes to fetch milk and bread. Are parks or community areas nearby? These might be needed if you start getting cabin fever during the witching hour.

- Schools – what's the catchment area like if you have a few nippers? Or if you are planning a family, it might be worthwhile checking out the neighbourhood for options, likewise for daycares. Again, like transportation, living in a good school catchment area is likely to also attract a premium for pricing.

Now that we are talking about schools and day care facilities, it's a good opportunity to speak about changing needs. Stuff happens, your needs will change and grow, nothing is really ever set in stone. Therefore, is there enough room for an expanding family? A change of jobs? All are potential events to consider. Remember though it's called a "first home" for a reason. It doesn't need to be the "be all and end all."

Types of options available

Broadly your dream home and where it lies geographically will be in one of two areas:

1. Inner city – within 10kms of a major urban area

2. City fringes/regional areas – outside the 10km radius.

Affordability and lifestyle preferences will be the two biggest deciding factors in where you choose to live. Cost is the biggest hurdle in securing a property within a close proximity of major urban areas. If location and proximity are key, and the budget is tight, be mindful that some compromises will be required.

Within these two broad buying regions, five main options will exist:

1. Existing 'detached' house
2. Existing unit/townhouse
3. Buying an off-the-plan house / unit / townhouse
4. Home and land packages
5. Buying land and building yourself.

Depending on your circumstances, all of the above can be fine choices. With each of these options, consideration should be given to the following:

- Know where you are buying and understand the dynamics of the location. What has the price growth in the region been for the past 10 or so years? Assess amenities and planned infrastructure developments and their potential effects on your investment. Pay attention to how many developments are also planned for the area as a lot of apartments coming on to the market at the same time will lead to oversupply and a decline in price growth.

- What are the zoning areas and any potential building restrictions? What do the Council/ Government have in store for future infrastructure projects? You don't want to find that your home will backing on to a major arterial road in the next few years!

- Don't ignore inspections and don't freak out over a bad one either. Inspectors will err on the side of caution largely to indemnify themselves. Therefore, carefully weighing up each of the variables as defects could also lead to a renegotiation. On the flipside, you don't want to be bedazzled and look at everything through rose coloured glasses.

- Be cautious with short financing periods.

- What's the neighbourhood like, how much noise is there (dogs, cars or ferals hanging around), what are the amenities, where are the schools and what is it like at different times of the day? The list is endless so try not to get analysis paralysis but be thorough and properly vet the property.

- Have proper searches conducted on the boundary lines and ensure the property in unencumbered.

- Costs, there are heaps of them so ensure you are on top of your finances.

- Insurance is one to watch. Happen to live in a flood plain? Not only will it really suck when it floods but insurance premiums will also go through the roof. Queenslanders know all about this one!

Existing Home

	PROS	CONS
Existing Property	▪ You know what you are getting. ▪ The look and touch factor is there. ▪ Infrastructure and amenities are in place.	▪ Might be time consuming to find and secure exactly what you want. ▪ It could require maintenance or improvements. ▪ Location and affordability particularly for free standing houses could restrict options.

Selection and comparison are the key factors that work in an existing homes benefit. They are already 'physically' present meaning they can be seen, touched and your imagination can wander on what your magic wand could do to spruce it up to your liking. Existing homes are usually in well developed areas meaning that the necessary amenities are close by. Being established also will tend to favour residences that are closer to major urban areas, with most experiencing strong demand and good capital growth prospects.

As existing homes will often be older, maintenance and repairs should be expected.

This is both an advantage and disadvantage as it gives you the chance to tailor the home to your liking and perhaps even help your haggling ability at the negotiation table. Disadvantages of course will include the expenditure outlay to rectify ageing issues down the track. Building inspection reports will uncover faults and defects to structures. They are undoubtedly worth doing in order to make an informed decision.

If you chose to go down an extensive remodelling process, ensure that the appropriate approvals are in place and consider the timelines involved.

Competition for quality existing homes in good locations will be high. Whilst it may be competitive and take a period of time to source and secure the 'ideal' place, it is realistically the path of least resistance in that, once the contract is signed, settlement and transfer of titles can be achieved in less than 30 days. This means that you will be in your home sooner. Patience in the search phase could pay handsome dividends in the long run.

Another disadvantage for first home buyers buying an existing home is that in most states the Home Buyers Grants are only available on newly constructed properties. This means that if you pursue this avenue, you could forfeit your ability to apply for the Grant.

Working at your own pace and deciding when the time is right will also work in your favour as you don't need to feel forced into making decisions until you are ready.

Existing Unit/Townhouse

An inner city unit could be a useful consideration for the astute first home buyer. Over the long–term, a decent growth rate could be expected, if you buy right. Major facilities will be close by and the luxury of multiple transportation routes could be at your doorstep. You may even be able to walk to work, if you're lucky.

Community living does mean community costs. Your contribution to the building upkeep can be expensive and it's another additional cost on top of your rates and utilities. An overly active body corporate can either be great or incredibly annoying. The two aspects you'll be contributing to are the Administrative and Sinking Fund.

The Admin fund covers the recurring costs of the building like electricity, insurance, cleaning and gardening fees. Sinking funds are for irregular costs like major building improvements that could take place. Lift upgrades, painting and / or construction activities will be covered by the sinking fund. The levies paid each year will be agreed upon at the Body Corporate Annual General Meeting. Work proposed through the use of the sinking fund or increases to levies for improvements will need to be voted on and a majority outcome will influence the decision. Some major unforeseen repairs may arise during the year and necessitate considerable outlays.

General considerations:

1. Chose a property that is individually metered so that it can be billed separately. It's not really fair when you pay the same water and gas as a single person, compared to the four-person family a few levels up. Newer buildings will tend to be individually metered though.

2. Where body corporates are established. Take the time to do searches and get the low down on what's been happening in the community of perhaps three dozen people. Having a Strata Inspection report completed should cover this off. Obtain a copy of the by-laws too. Otherwise you could end up finding that your puppy can't also come live with you.

3. Body corporate fees - don't forget about them as they'll pop up every quarter. The money will keep the gardens nice, the pool cleaned, and cover insurance and administration.

4. Proposed maintenance or upgrades. Plans may have been in motion for 18 months and you've just entered the new apartment only to find you'll be slugged

an extra $2k a quarter because they are painting the building outside, all 20 stories, and the lift is getting an upgrade. This information will come up through the review of the Strata Report.

5. Will you be able to become an active participant in the building's management? Volunteering your services for the body corporate could be time-consuming and political, particularly if money has to be spent. Everyone has an opinion and motivations will differ. But it will give you more influence to achieve outcomes. Plus, it could be a good way to give back to the community.

6. Check the boundaries - where does your property actually start and finish before "common areas" start.

7. In older buildings avoid asbestos. Also, for an older building, will it handle 21st century technology? Consider how hard it might be to hook up the NBN or Foxtel etc.

8. Location, location, location. Hunt for areas that have height restrictions as it could prevent a 100 unit development going up next door. The land is still worth money and you own that dirt. Owning one unit in ten is much better than one in 100, if it is the same sized block. Go for appeal; don't choose something that looks at a brick wall.

Buying off the plan unit/townhouse

	PROS	CONS
Off the Plan	• Time. Time to save, time to secure finance. • Putting a deposit down 'locks in' the price. The property could also appreciate in value once it's completed. Today's prices at tomorrow's value. • Home buyers' incentives and concessions. • Builders guarantee – in Australia newly built properties come with a seven year guarantee on structural and interior defects.	• Time. The project might run over time and have extensive and potentially costly delays. • No touch and feel factor. It may not turn out as you imagined. • Might not go ahead – if a developer doesn't secure enough upfront sales, the project could be mothballed.

New development releases will often be priced lower in order to draw the punters in and this helps secure the project's future, meaning they'll complete the task as they have secured upfront dollars to make it possible. Getting involved at this stage could be worth your while because of:

1. Good pricing.

2. Equity – you can lock in the property without having to settle for an extended period. Capital growth in that period can

make that deposit quite valuable. But remember, prices don't always go up. Choose wisely.

3. Time – a longer settlement. Allows you to take stock, work towards something and source additional funds.

4. Government chips in – there could be Stamp Duty concessions on the new build and additional money in the pot with your First Home Buyers Grant. Getting in early allows you to cherry pick from the best development options. Obviously, there are some great benefits to be had but off-the-plan developments are complex stuff. Therefore do the following checks as a minimum:

    o   It is very important when buying off the plan that you go with a reputable developer. Check out their past work, vet them through feedback channels, do license checks, check out previous disciplinary actions etc. If your research turns up anything concerning, maybe reconsider. Gain an understanding of their financial situation because if they go bust, it could mean an unfinished project and your deposit tied up in an abyss for a long time.

○ Getting finance can be sometimes a little tougher in this scenario. Lenders may cap the Loan to Value Ratio (LVR we will cover this off in more detail later), or may require later approval on completion. Choose wisely, visualise the look and feel, check the paperwork and get advice.

○ Potential increase in value once completed. What you visualise, and what eventuates could be quite different. Consider your favourite book and the result after they have made it into a movie. It may have all the bits and bobs but it just wasn't quite right. What you should really consider is whether or not the numbers actually stack up, how likely the developer/builder is to deliver against their promises and whether contractually it's in your favour.

Sellers/developers will promise that you are buying tomorrow's real estate for today's prices. This could well be the case. It's just as possible for it not to be the case. To truly nail buying off-the-plan, the key is understanding every aspect of the contract prior to signing. Therefore:

▪ I would recommend as a necessity that the contract be reviewed by a lawyer to determine financial details and what commitments are required should the project run over time. If it is a display house/ unit, it could be worthwhile having an architect review the property to give you a more accurate assessment of what you are buying. Make sure everything is detailed in the contract, right down to the appliance and fitting/fixture types. Be sure to question if there are any discrepancy on what you receive and what has contractually been committed to.

- Are binding strata title contracts in place? Again have these reviewed by a lawyer to ensure fair terms have been agreed.

- New developments in in-demand areas will often be heavily marketed to attract a premium. This marketing will only be added into the cost. Question marketing that offers rental guarantees because it could be a signal that the developer feels there could be an oversupply hence pushing down the value. Costs are built into prices so evaluate any contractual aspect that could draw you into additional expense requirements.

Others factors to consider before signing on the bottom line:

- Again, location, location, location. What noise is there? Is it in a new suburb? Is the necessary infrastructure in place?

- Imagine the living spaces and the outlook you'll potentially have. How much space will you actually have? Consider where you will store your things. Buying an 80sqm apartment 'off the plan' with two bedrooms, two bathrooms, separate lounge, kitchen will likely be a pretty pokey space. Try and visualise or find something comparable and existing just to give you a better idea. Also, can it be customised to get it to your exact liking?

- Does the developer have all the necessary Local Council approvals already in place?

- Have a contingency plan. And finances need to be planned accordingly. Valuations will be required by the bank upon completion of the build. If the valuation is lower than the contract price you will need a back-up plan to cover the discrepancy of the Loan to Value Ratio.

- Ummm... where are you planning on living while it is getting built?

- What if the property isn't completed on time? What are you going to do? Can you afford to continue putting money into rent?

- Stamp Duty and other concessions may be available in your state so make sure you complete the necessary checks and get every cent you are entitled to.

- It's great to have time on your side to save so make sure it's used properly. Procrastinating and delaying budgeting will hurt when the time comes to finalise your finances.

- Always question everything and ensure you understand what you are entering into.

House and land package (detached buying off the plan)

Getting a package deal can be a bit like pulling a house off a production line, but it comes with a long list of options including colours, doorknobs, land choices and, so much more. The list is really endless. Once again buying off the plan can be a great option because of the time parameters. Time to save, time for capital growth, time to get grants approved, and time to just generally get things in order.

Depending on the location, you may get great "bang for your buck" in new housing developments. Decent block sizes, completely new dwellings designed to your liking/taste, plus incentives/concessions in the form of buyer's grants and stamp duty may all be possible. You can even "go green" and save thousands on utility costs over the long-term – there's a lot going for it. Long-term capital growth will likely be achieved because others will come into the area and this will increase infrastructure and services.

Developers are very in tune to the popularity of this and are quick to snap up new land releases for planned communities. Generally, a developer will build the houses and on-sell them or provide a choice of lots and a number of customised house packages which can then be tailored to your liking.

Financing in this arrangement is usually a little different as you'll have the loan for the land and a separate construction loan. The construction loan is drawn down on for progress payments to be met for the builder. Upon completion the loans will be brought together. A benefit during this time is that you are only paying interest on the sums drawn down on not the entire amount straight away.

Contracts can be fixed in agreement which is beneficial in maintaining the risk of a budget blow out. The trick is in determining what is actually included in this fixed contract. Different builders will have different inclusions (they each make their money in different ways) so you really need to understand want you are getting for your money. Fencing, appliances, painting, gardening: are any of those included? Similarly to buy off the plan – the contract is King! In the contract you will also want to ensure there are guarantees on structural aspects and warranties for goods.   Therefore, I have to stress the importance of due diligence, doing your research, visiting past work, taking references and whatever else you feel is needed to make an informed decision.

We have spoken about the body corporate previously, however they can also apply in situations outside your normal apartment block complex. New housing developments may also incorporate a body corporate levy. This could be to maintain common areas in the estate and facilities. A "green" estate that generates power off the grid may impose a levy for maintenance and for the upkeep of equipment. Likewise, for shared water treatment facilities. Again, great concepts but when problems arises they could be costly.

Buying land and building yourself

	PROS	CONS
New build (DIY)	• It's new. It's bright. It's shiny. • Designed to your specifications and requirements. Adding to the sentimental factors. • Home buyer's incentives.	• Construction delays and mishaps can be costly. • Going through a Local Council building approval process can be time consuming and difficult. • Disputes with builders over contracts. It can be pretty stressful.

You've searched high and low and just cannot find something that's 'you'! The big attraction of building is that you have the opportunity to create something that is fit for your purposes and needs. Something that you feel can become an extension of yourself.

It begins with the sourcing and procurement of the land. Next comes getting plans drawn up and getting them through a Local Council building approval process. There is the potential to have delays at each stage of the process. Budget blowouts are particularly common. The costs of building a home are generally fraught with unaccounted expenses. Fitting, features and gardening will all be on-costs so be very mindful of what the true completion cost will be.

Tip – you won't receive the First Home Buyer Grant (FHBG) if you have only bought land. A comprehensive building contract will be required as well in order to claim the grant.

Consider these four points of your dream house as they will have a huge impact on the total cost of the build:

1. Cost of the land and landscaping
2. Overall size
3. Interior and exterior finishes
4. Amenities (creature comforts).

Blocks can often be priced almost the same in

new land releases, with slightly higher costs usually associated with slightly larger or more level blocks. However, construction costs can vary significantly, due to sloping or odd-shaped blocks which can have a big impact on cost because of the preparation and groundwork required prior to construction. Ideally, the house should suit the block as opposed to forcing a house plan that isn't fit for purpose. When choosing a block, you would want to ensure it is zoned for residential purposes and that there aren't restrictions (easements) which could cause a headache or two when the plans are getting approved. Drainage and fire protection are also aspects to factor in. Smaller blocks are likely to mean higher density housing which could impact on privacy and the serenity you hoped to create.

Also what is the true cost of the location? Cheaper housing on the city fringe is balanced by continuing higher transport costs (car price, fuel, maintenance, time). There is a trade-off but is the daily commute to work also worth it?

Obviously the larger the house build, the more it will cost because of the additional use of materials required. Interior and exterior finishes will impact significantly on cost and, when it comes to building, the sky is really the limit. Not only will there be upfront costs but you need to be mindful that a bigger house will mean bigger utilities' bills for heating, cooling and lighting.

Considering putting in a pool? An additional bathroom? The amenities you chose will have a big impact on the overall feel of the place and again the more add-ons you chose, the bigger the construction bill will be. Looking outside your home, what is happening in the surrounding suburb? What future facilities are being planned? What mobile, internet and TV coverage is available is also another consideration.

Importantly, the same conditions apply to buying off-the-plan in that the contract is king. Sourcing a builder and a good one at that will be worth their weight in gold. Top builders need to be consultative, produce quality work and manage a fine line between being consultative but also not hassling you with minor problems that arise on a daily basis. Your contract will cover off the specifics of what is actually included. Generally, it won't be enough to have 100% completeness. What fittings and fixtures are included, what impacts will material changes have on the bottom line, who will be sourcing trades and what level of autonomy will you provide the builder? Are you intending to be on site daily to check progress and participate in the project management process? Will the builder even allow this?

Planning your attack

The home buying process commences by getting your own finances in order, first and foremost. Affordability and the time required to save an initial deposit are the two biggest initial obstacles to overcome so you will need to adopt some financial discipline, pay off niggling debts and concentrate on growing that nest egg.

Second comes research and doing the due diligence on the ideal home you want to secure. Obviously this can be done concurrently with the saving and budgeting regime. Obtaining pre-approval on your home loan is next and, once achieved, you're well on your way to owning your home.

Sourcing, negotiating and securing the property are next, followed by closing out the process by doing the contracts and closing out the finance.

And lastly is moving in to enjoy your new cave or castle.

Sounds simple when laid out over a few pages but, as we all know, the devil is in the detail. In the following chapters, we will explore each of these aspects in detail, providing you enough information to make you dangerous in a competitive housing market.

KEY CHAPTER POINTS:

1. Buy when you are ready, when it is what you want and when it fits your current stage of life.

2. Consider all of your options and choose the one that feels right for you. House, unit, off-the- plan, renting, house-sharing etc. are all great options depending on your circumstances and needs at any particular time in your life.

3. The housing market fluctuates like the weather seasons – from hot to cold and warm to chilly. Buyers' markets could give you the best bang for your buck. However, a good buy can be found under any type of weather conditions.

4. Time is the aspect that favours buying over renting. Time will allow you to pay off the debt. Time also provides an opportunity for capital growth.

5. Affordability and saving for an initial deposit can tend to be the biggest battles you'll initially face.

6. Visualise what you're ideal home looks like and consider what particular amenities you will need.

7. Buying an existing home allows you to work at your own pace, and the physical presence gives assurance on what you are getting into. Maintenance and future improvements may be required.

41

8. Existing units/townhouses will have body corporate fees, and additional research is required to understand commitments to levies and sinking funds.

9. The contract is king when it comes to building or buying off-the-plan. Understanding what you are entering into helps ensure that 'nasty surprises' don't pop up.

10. Building your dream home or starter home can be challenging and you must always build to suit the block. Keep a very close eye on costs. Again, watch the contract.

11. Understand what you are getting in to. All contracts are complex stuff, so review, seek legal advice and ask a lot of questions.

SAVING

Saving for that initial deposit is more than half of the battle, especially when it is so easy to be frivolous and to maintain your current habits. Your habits are your pattern, but if you want to own bricks and mortar, changing your spending pattern is the hardest and arguably the most important undertaking you will make. Setting a good foundation and establishing good habits will be hugely beneficial for you in the long run.

I have a confession... I went on a Contiki trip and it was six weeks of alcohol fuelled fun. Came home feeling like a man of the world but it took me two years to pay off my holiday debt. Such a scenario is not unique just to me. Others have taken overseas holidays, accumulated additional personal debt, used the credit card more often than they realised and then had car loan repayments on top of that. Suddenly half the weekly wage has been blown.

When you're faced with multiple concurrent debts, it can be crippling and all-too-easy to say "it's all just too hard." Killing debt is paramount and no effective saving strategy includes debt repayments. The reason behind this is that interest on debt will always be higher than the amount you'll receive by keeping your cash in the bank. The sooner the debt has gone, the sooner you'll start breathing easier.

A short and simple introduction to debt

- Identifying debt and types of debt

- Facts about debt
- Debt management strategies

Debt is common place, so common in fact that almost everyone has it in one form or another. There is nothing to be embarrassed by having it. And it will only become unmanageable when it is ignored and/or goes beyond your means. Managing and maintaining your debt is easy to do when you actually understand what it is all about. By understanding why things are the way they are, you can find easy solutions to overcome your own individual debt problems.

Identifying debt and types of debt

Unfortunately, not all debts are created equal. Debts would be so much easier to manage if they were. Understanding the subtle differences is critical to determining which one to tackle first. Increased understanding allows a bit of strategy to come in to play as opposed to making sporadic payments here and there to multiple outstanding lenders. In its most basic form, debt can be broken down into three areas:

1. Is it secured or unsecured?

   Secured debt means "collateral" is tied up in the arrangement. Collateral is security and held against the debt. For example, if you had a car loan, your car would be used as "collateral" in case you defaulted on the loan. It's like a ransom.

Unsecured debt is the opposite in that no collateral is held against it. A credit card is a fine example of an unsecured debt. An unsecured debt is more likely to attract a higher rate of interest because it is a "riskier" loan for the lender compared to a secured debt.

2. How the debt is paid – structured or unstructured?

A structured debt will have a timeline for installment payments. Again, a car loan would be a good example. The big benefit in this scenario is that there are no surprises as the repayment amounts and timeline are fixed or known.

Credit cards are unstructured debts because they don't have a fixed payment amount. A minimum repayment will be calculated by taking a small percentage of the amount owing plus interest. This is where the debt gets troublesome because you have the option to "pay the minimum" or "pay more" – and having the option can lead to people getting caught up in the "we'll just pay for it next month" mindset.

3. Debt source – who actually holds the debt?

Who is the source? The source of where the debt/money came from is a huge indicator in choosing which one to pay off first. The source with the highest interest rate is the one that has to go first!

Typical Debt	Secured/ Unsecured	Structured/ Unstructured	Typical Source
Car loan	Secured	Structured	Bank
Personal loan	Unsecured	Structured	Bank
Credit/Store card	Unsecured	Unstructured	Bank/Credit Institution
Investment	Secured	Structured	Bank
Payday loans	Unsecured	Structured	Credit agency/ loan shark
Cash advance	Unsecured	Structured/ Unstructured	Credit agency/ Mum & Dad/ Loan Shark
Study/Tuition	Unsecured (and is considered an investment debt)	Structured	Government under the HECS Scheme

Facts about debt

The Australian Government struggles to balance the books and media outlets bash up debt problems regularly. Debt is a dirty secret that everyone has and yet rarely openly talks about. It's like hearing about a gambler's wins but never their loses.

To put this into perspective, according to the Australian Bureau of Statistics, Government debt floats somewhere between 12-14% of our Gross Domestic Product (GDP), whereas household debt is in the vicinity of 100% of GDP. At the end of 2013 household debt was in excess of $1.8 trillion or about 80 grand for every Australian. Pretty big number, huh? Now I won't argue about the semantics and social issues that this topic could uncover but the numbers speak for themselves. And it is consistent, we all have it and are sometimes a little scared about it, but in the end we have to deal with it.

The true fact about debt is that the only way we can reduce it is by:

1. earning more, or
2. spending less.

Earning more isn't always that easy, especially over the short-to-medium term. Spending less can be done with immediate effect. This is what we will now explore further.

Debt management strategies

Tighten the belt, cut up the credit cards, remove all of life's luxuries including the morning coffee and you can only eat beans. That's my hot tip! Doesn't sound like much fun and taking an approach like that isn't likely to last long. You'll find that your emotions are directly linked to budgeting and saving. You feel glum, a shopping spree can help but afterwards you feel remorseful for blowing your plan and going back to square one. A debt strategy needs to be realistic because cutting it to the bones can work for some but you don't want to be resentful of it either.

So first and foremost take responsibility for your debt. How it ever happened, this is the debt you created... so onwards and upwards. Next point is to pick where to start. The most common way to debt diet is:

- Consolidating
- Aggressively paying down
- Goal setting
- **Budgeting.**

Consolidating

Obtaining a debt consolidation loan will urge all of your existing loans and credit cards into a single loan. The larger the total amount though, the harder it will be to consolidate.

Credit card transfers can be viewed from a consolidation perspective. The rates are attractive and the rates could be 0% for an 18 or 24 month period. Very tempting! Worthwhile if you can pay off the loan in that interest-free period. Not worthwhile if you can't as you'll end up accumulating more.

Note – if a new loan has a lower interest rate than the interest on your highest rate loan, then it's pretty likely you'll save money. What you really need to watch is the fees of establishing and exiting this arrangement because this is where you could come unstuck. Fixed rate loans may also attract fees if you pay out the loan early; this is sometimes referred to as a "repayment adjustment." Also, you might find that the repayment period has extended, which could result in a lower installment payment but it will take longer to pay off. Again, costing more... Do the math!

Aggressive paying down

It's a basic, "cut it to the bones" type strategy. Cut down all variable spending to the minimum and just go hell-for-leather on putting as much extra money into those debts. Move home, sell the car and walk, get a second job, keep entertainment to a minimum and when you do go out, don't over-spend and sometimes ask your closest friends to shout you a beer/ meal/ ticket. (Then when things pick up, you will "owe them one" in return). This will be tough going and might make you resentful so perhaps just try it for a period of time and have a short spell of loosening the reins as a reward. Like a "Dry July" or a "Cheapskate June."

Goal setting

Goals force you to take direction and change your pattern of current behaviour. The best goals are the ones that are achieved by continually focusing your attention on them. Don't make goals that are a reaction to circumstances or designed to get away from things you don't want. Create goals that are a realistic stretch, that force a bit of tension in your life, that are clear, concise and focused on creating your vision.

A goal should be something like:

To pay off $7,000 of credit card debt within the next six months by contributing an additional $270 per week on top of my monthly repayment.

This is a good goal as it is clear, concise and time-specific.

Paying a debt off, saving a deposit, getting that job promotion etc. isn't down to luck but you and your own efforts. Whatever actions you take, will result in the end result to match. Consistency is the key or else you will tend to swing between having what you want and not achieving anything. Focusing on consistency allows you to achieve your goals in perpetuity. "Stick-to-itiveness" is a personal favourite made up word. In that when you create realistic goals and stick to them, results will be achieved.

Exercise:

Write down three simple financial goals you would like to achieve in the next six months:

1. _____
2. _____
3. _____

Two quick potential considerations:

Can you sell something to pay your debts off? Can you downsize/reduce/go without? Gumtree and eBay are great sites to get rid of unwanted items. Clean out the garage or storage cupboard of all your unwanted goods and convert them into some cash.

Can you get a part-time job? Do a little something on the side? Do you have a creative flair or an artistic talent? Try websites like www.elance.com or www.freelancer.com or www.fiverr.com – there are a lot of these sites out there. People sell their skills and you take can on jobs worldwide. Writers, artists, designers, programmers, editors, mathematicians, tutors etc. all bid on different work gigs. Try participating in surveys which pay. For the alternative thinkers out there, come up with an easy-to-do service. For example, on fivver.com people charge to be others online girlfriend or boyfriend. Or offer a service for $10 to write three individual comments on a specialised blog post. That's pretty easy stuff, so use your creativity to spin a buck or two.

TIP ➜ Check your credit rating! Refer to www.mycreditlife.com.au and know what you're up against when you are facing a lender. Be on the front foot so that there are no surprises.

Budgeting

Budgeting is so important it gets its own separate section! To commence, let's get to know your weekly spending habits. Start by doing a brain dump, listing your income and all of your expenses that immediately spring to mind. The morning coffee, rent, phone bill/s, social outings, hobbies and everything else in between. We'll get into the detail but let's make a small start... Start listing:

Looking at your spending habits tends to be alarming, perhaps because it's all on paper and able to be examined. Budgets allow you decide what you can cut, which is really the next part of the problem. Saving for a deposit doesn't mean that you cannot have a good lifestyle. But cutting back a little and making some sacrifices might not be such a bad thing, especially when there will be a long-term reward.

Now, I won't lecture you on what you should and shouldn't cut. It's your life, and your choice.

Everyone's personal circumstances and journey will be different but we all face the same battle of keeping our finances healthy and, at times, getting the budget back in the black.

OK, decision time and this is where it could start getting ugly. Answer the big question: what can be realistically cut and scaled back or are there cheaper alternatives? What you decide is up to you but be realistic and don't cut it to the bones. Cutting back too far will just make you annoyed or even resentful and could ultimately steer you away from your desired course.

Budgeting and planning are largely about control, being honest and laying out your expenses. Always try to overestimate. That way, you'll always have a little extra to play with. If you have no idea of what you are actually spending and on what, pull out your iPhone and download a free expense monitoring app. If you don't have a smartphone, invest in a $2 dollar notepad to record what you actually spend over a day, week, fortnight and month. The results tend to be quite scary. When I first did it, I actually realised how undisciplined I was. Had a great lifestyle but I lived month-to-month with nothing to show for it.

The devil is in the detail so now let's set it all out as it stands today and get on top of your household balance sheet. The important thing is to be honest with your figures.

Exercise:

INCOME	FREQUENCY	AMOUNT PER MONTH
Take home pay		
Income from savings/ investments		
Government benefits		
Family benefit payments		
Other – sources of real funds that you receive regularly		
TOTAL		

** Honesty is the absolute best policy – no overestimates in the income section.

Expenses

COMMITMENTS	FREQUENCY	AMOUNT PER MONTH
Rent		
Insurance		
Car insurance		
Health insurance		
Car registration		
Other		
Total		

UTILITIES	FREQUENCY	AMOUNT PER MONTH
Electricity		
Gas		
Water		
Internet		
Pay TV		
Phone		
Total		
EDUCATION	FREQUENCY	AMOUNT PER MONTH
Child care/preschool		
School uniforms		
Stationary, music etc		
Excursions/ camps		
HECS/Tertiary debt		
Other		
Total		
HEALTH	FREQUENCY	AMOUNT PER MONTH
Doctor		
Dentist		
Medicine		
Eye care/glasses		
Vet		
Other		
Total		

SHOPPING	FREQUENCY	AMOUNT PER MONTH
Supermarket		
Fruit/veggies		
Baby products		
Clothes/shoes		
Cosmetics/toiletries		
Gifts		
Other		
Total		
TRANSPORT	FREQUENCY	AMOUNT PER MONTH
Car maintenance		
Fuel		
Tolls/parking		
Taxis		
Other		
Total		
ENTERTAINMENT	FREQUENCY	AMOUNT PER MONTH
Holiday		
Pub/club		
Gym memberships		
Movies		
Hobbies		
TAB/Sports bet		

Restaurants		
Take away / Lunches / Dinners		
Regular coffee/tea		
Other		
Total		
OTHER	FREQUENCY	AMOUNT <u>PER MONTH</u>
Credit/ Store Card Repayment		
Fees/ Charges		
Personal loan		
TOTAL INCOME		

Minus

Total Commitments	
Total Utilities	
Education	
Health	
Shopping	
Transport	
Entertainment	
Other	
TOTAL EXPENSES	

** This is by no means an exhaustive list. The additional space is there for your use. Please tweak wherever necessary to tailor it to your specific needs.

Also refer to www.thebuyersguide.com.au for singles, couples or family budgets.

Total Income VS Total Expenses = ?

Give yourself a pat on the back if you have been honest and, for wading through it all. Now though, the important bit, is there any money left over? Or are you in the red?

Don't worry; whatever the results, it's ok for the time being. You now know what you are dealing with. Look through your budget now and decide what can be cut. What can you spend less on? Can you negotiate? Can you shop around for a better deal?

Keep tweaking this budget until you can realistically create a week-to-week surplus. The first thing to remember is: any surplus is a good surplus, and it's a start! The second thing to remember is that starting the process is the hardest. So don't delay, get to it.

You can find out more about saving and reducing spending at www.thebuyersguide .com.au along with additional exercises, budgeting tools and helpful resources.

Remember we are putting this plan together for the simple reason of moving you away from living paycheck-to-paycheck. I know it's hard but the challenge is starting and then stick-to-itiveness!!

There are many variations on these key common strategies. Variations are the result of personal circumstances. A single working Mum's preferred strategy is likely to be a lot different to the "DINK's" living down the road. Whatever you do, don't be embarrassed by debt, as everyone has it. The embarrassing part is when you ignore it. Don't let it get hold of you and if it starts to, don't let it deteriorate further. Speak with your lenders, let them know your situation immediately, seek advice and work with your lenders to develop an alternative payment plan.

The market has a lot to offer for your debts, all with big promises. Tread lightly, assess your options, do the numbers and seek advice where possible. The best course is the simplest – budget carefully, create a surplus each week/ month/ year and put it into the debt with the highest interest rate first. Aggressively paying off debts will likely mean many scarifies but the discipline you build now will pay big dividends in time to come.

Saving

We've all tried to save at one point or another but something tends to always pop up. Bit like getting back to the gym after a long time off. First, you think about doing it. Next, you'll talk about doing it. Then you'll complain about how hard it is, only to finally give up or succumb to temptation.

But now that we have an awareness of our debts, and a budget in place that we are going to stick to, the next aspect is cutting costs wherever possible, just to get that little bit further again. There are millions of ways to save money, some are extreme, and some aren't worth the time and energy. But a dollar is a dollar so, without further ado, here are **The Buyers Guide** best saving tips to kick those frivolous spending habits:

- Start by establishing a separate savings account. Maximise this by taking it out of your day-to-day low interest bank account. Check out alternatives like high-interest e-accounts or bonus savers which tend to offer higher returns and the capital is guaranteed.

- Save your change. Get a tin and at the end of each day pop in any loose coins. If you're really keen, also include your $5 notes. A little change here and there quickly adds up. Best of all, you won't miss it.

- Allocate 10% of your wage directly to savings. Ask HR or the Accounts department to divide your paycheck into separate accounts. On payday, it will initially seem a bit light but with a good budget in place you'll get by.

- Look for banking accounts with no fees or ATM charges. Seems simple but keep track of your account and how much you actually have in it. Do you decline an ATM receipt because you're scared to look at your cash balance? Take a set amount of cash out on Monday and once it's done for the week, it's done.

- Stop smoking, cut back on alcohol and when you're feeling stressed, take a brisk walk. A healthy attitude to life is much cheaper!

- Take shorter showers, turn off the lights and switch off appliances. Simple things add up. Also, don't leave the air conditioner on.

- Heading out for a night on the town? Get the bus/ train/ ferry instead of a taxi. Or have a party at home instead. If you fancy a punt, hold a poker night. Hosting a dinner party? Why not make it a pot-luck dinner where everyone contributes their own dish. If you and your friends are bad cooks, go to your favourite cheap BYO restaurant and later call an early night or be the designated driver.

- Become a hunter – a specials' hunter. Plan your meals! Only buy what you need and go for the generic brands. Don't be fooled by the two-for-$5 deals or anything else that is in bright, shiny lights. Never go grocery-shopping hungry and buy based on value not price.

- Stop, pause, and repeat. Thinking of making an unnecessary purchase? Wait

30 days and if you are still keen, then go for it.

- Credit cards are fine if you pay them off in the interest-free period. If this can't be managed, cut them up! WHAT, you say! I really mean it!

- Pay cash wherever possible as it will cut back on unnecessary purchases and, what's more, reward schemes aren't worth shit! 60,000 points for a set of movie tickets... puh-lease!

- Drink water instead of soft drink, eat frozen veggies rather than buying fresh produce, and remember cheap cuts of meat in the slow cooker are always tastier. If you have a green thumb, that's even better. Start your own veggie patch or window pot... a couple of herbs, cherry tomatoes and whatever else that will grow with a little attention and off you go.

- Cost conscious single lady? Date more.

- Cost conscious single man? Be creative. If you can't, go see Mum, Grandma, Aunty Betty or anyone else that will give you a free feed.

- Get rid of your landline. Seriously, who calls on a landline other than telemarketers anyway?

- Become a second-hand man/ lady. Great stuff is available through online classifieds and seconds stores. Awesome way to clear out some junk as well. Remember: it's someone else's treasure. If you're keen, kerbside pick-ups might be worth investigating. Have a garage sale or go on treasure hunts and try and flip the item for a profit on eBay or Gumtree.

- Shop around for discounts on your bills. Check out comparison sites for the best deals. If you have Contents, Car and Third Party Insurance shop around because most insurers will offer you a multi policy discount... straight up.

- Thinking about an expensive weekend getaway? Why not give back to the community instead? Volunteer at a local charity and develop some different perspectives.

- Ask for a pay raise. Be bold; speak of your recent achievements and the benefit that you bring to the business. If you don't get cash, ask for other benefits that could help over the long-term, like further training and development.

- Ask for discounts, ask for fees to be waived and ask for upgrades. You don't need to be a smart-arse about it, but if you don't chance your hand, you'll never know.

- If you can't give up the treats (beer, ciggies, shopping etc.) be disciplined and save the same amount as the purchased item. Put it directly into paying off a debt.

- Divide up your regular monthly expenses into envelopes so there aren't any surprises when the bills come in.

- Look out for worthwhile reward programs, use shop-a-dockets and entertainment vouchers.

- Lasagne. Cook up a big batch on a Sunday afternoon and literally that casserole dish will last all week. Or at least feed a family for a good couple of nights.

- Don't spend money to de-stress. Do some deep breathing, exercise, mediate, give a boxing bag hell. If you don't own one, put your mattress against the wall and give that hell instead.

- Live in a cheaper place or area.

- What's on in your city... there are always free events on, so find something of interest for you. Nature is the best free source of entertainment so have a lazy day on the beach, hike up a bush trail, explore a new park. There is plenty to do out there.

- Give travelling and holidays a miss. Don't worry, it will still be there next time when you can truly afford to go.

Ultimately, a long-term consistent strategy is what truly works best. There will be people who will promise to pull a rabbit out a hat for you. But realistically the way to get ahead requires discipline and consistency over time.

Resources & Assistance

There are a lot of people, businesses and financial institutions out there that will be willing to help. The common theme though is that their help will come at a price. Now sometimes you do have to pay a little to get a better return and that's fine. Other times the deal can be loaded with temptation and potential traps, let alone additional fees and charges. In essence, be careful, READ THE CONTRACT, ask if you don't understand, seek an alternative opinion and sleep on it before making a decision. If you then feel it weighs up and will work for you, do it.

The Buyers Guide being completely independent will remain a trusted source of information. So stay tuned to our latest articles. The following sites are also worth investigating:

1. www.moneysmart.gov.au
2. www.simplesavings.com.au
3. www.financialcounsellingaustralia.org.au
4. www.debtselfhelp.org.au

All are no-fuss sources of information but if you do a simple Google search, a lot of information will come up about debt management services providers. Fees and charges will apply but if they get you on track, it might just be the encouragement you need.

If you are genuinely experiencing hardship, don't delay. Get on the phone or go to see your lenders or service providers (telephone, electricity, gas, water). Explain the circumstances and work with them to devise an alternative payment structure. It is a legal requirement for providers to develop an alternative payment structure should you be experiencing hardship. Differing or reducing repayments or altering the loan repayment term could potentially be arranged. Don't delay because the sooner you address your debt problem, the more options will be available. Another good website to reference is – www.doingittough.info which provides tips and helps identify when you're experiencing hardship.

Borrowing more to get out of debt is a slippery slope and fraught with danger. It is best avoided at all cost (no pun intended).

Alternative options - Investments

OK, you're on top of your budget and putting money aside is fairly easy but you're dissatisfied with cash attracting a relatively low rate in the bank. If you have a long- term timeframe, there are a couple of options to consider. Long-term is the key because you won't see results overnight and markets fluctuate so with time on your side perhaps look into these options:

Managed funds

Basically it is a pool of money that is managed by an investment/ fund manager. The fund manager will then invest in shares, cash, property and other assets on your behalf. A management fee will be charged and the value will rise and fall depending on the underlying asset values. Income will be generated which you can chose to take or reinvest.

Pros
They offer diversification and access to a wide invest base for a small initial investment.

Cons
You are relying on your fund manager's skills, and fees and charges will apply.

Direct equities – shares

This is like having direct ownership of a company, albeit only a very tiny proportion. Stocks, shares, equities – they are all the same, just known by different names. These can be a great long-term investment but you will be much more exposed to the volatility of the trading market.

Pros
Income and growth potential. As a share owner of a business, you are directly invested in their fortune so when business is good, you'll receive dividends (income) and an increase in share values.

Cons
Share prices fluctuate a lot and can trend downwards to zero! The main downside is the risk you are exposed to.

Index funds

These are similar to a managed fund in that you buy a series of assets that mirror an index – be it industrial, gold, iron, banking etc.

Pros
There is an element of diversification as you're investing in multiple businesses in the index. Therefore, the risk is spread.

Cons
There are not a huge amount of Index fund options available in which to invest, particularly in comparison to managed funds, for example.

Term deposits

This is a simple form of investment that will generally attract a higher rate of interest than a day-to-day account because it is held for a 'term'. The pre-determined term could vary from one month to five years.

Pros
Low risk investment and fixed interest returns are guaranteed for the term.

Cons

Accessing your money during the term period will be difficult and penalties may apply if you break the term.

With any investment, there are risks involved. Markets will always fluctuate, and the best strategy is the one that is well-researched and thoroughly discussed with professionals who can help you to determine what is best for your unique circumstances.

KEY CHAPTER POINTS:

1. Killing debt is paramount as no effective saving strategy includes debt repayments. Also, once you are free from personal debt, don't accumulate new ones.

2. Debt is either 'secured' or 'unsecured', with the difference being that collateral is held as a 'security'. Unsecured debts, being the opposite, will likely attract a higher interest rate. Different debts will have different repayment terms. And the source of the debt will affect the amount of interest charged.

3. Consolidating debt will combine all your loans into one, meaning it has one interest rate and one repayment method. This strategy gives structure and can make you more aware of what you owe.

4. Aggressively paying off debt is a "cut to the bones" type of strategy. This can be hard to sustain as temptations are always around the corner.

5. Goals are best achieved when they are clear, concise and time-specific. What you continue to concentrate your attention on, you will end up achieving.

6. Budgeting is the ultimate tool to use to get on top of your finances. It is the household equivalent of a balance sheet. The devil is in the detail, decide what can be cut and most importantly stick-to-it!

71

7. There are thousands of ways to save money. Be creative and focus on the ways that work best for you.

8. If you are experiencing financial hardship be on the front foot and speak to your lenders about repayment strategies. Debt assistance companies are out there but they will charge fees for their services.

9. If you are on top of your debts and saving money easily, then maybe consider an investment to achieve a higher return, compared to having cash sitting in the bank. Investments only ever generate the best returns over the long-term and therefore seek professional advice prior to leaping into the deep end.

For additional assistance be sure to check out www.thebuyersguide.com.au

SECURING FINANCE

Money, money, money... it's all about the money. How much to get, when to get it, where to get it and who will give it to you are the aspects you will need to navigate. Usually a very daunting task for anyone. It is likely to be biggest investment that you've pursued to date and definitely one you must get right. The right decision is an informed decision so this section will cover off:

- Avenues to access finance
- Obtaining pre-approval and its importance
- How much to borrow
- How banks will assess your loan application and processes they will run through
- How long the application process will take
- Borrowing options that are available.

Avenues to access finance

Gone are the days of having to front-up to the bank manager to plead your case for a mortgage. It is a competitive market today and banks want your business. Mortgage brokers are just as keen to get your application in front of them as well.

Shop around yourself; this is a great way to learn what's available in the market. Visit the banks directly and see what deal you can broker directly. This process can take time and doesn't necessarily mean you'll secure the best deal. Alternatively, you can use a mortgage broker.

Mortgage brokers can do much of the leg work for you, plus there is a lot to take in and learn, so this is even more reason to use their services. Brokers have the ability to assess a range of products from multiple lenders. Therefore, they can help direct you to the right product for specific circumstances, which doesn't necessarily need to be the cheapest option. They chase and liaise with the bank, do the grunt admin and they receive their commission from the bank. They can process your First Home Buyers Grant, help with budgeting and they should possess good knowledge of options/ products available.

To get the best out of a broker, you should carefully assess their skills and what they can offer you. Some questions to ask include:

1. How do you decide what is best for me?
2. What impact will my personal debts have against my borrowing capacity?
3. What fees are involved?
4. What are the loan features?
5. What information do I need to provide?
6. Walk me through the steps... what is actually involved and what are the timelines?

7. Should I fix the rate or not?

8. Any other tips you can share?

9. Are you affiliated with any particular providers? What disclosure will you provide?

10. Can you explain that again? ☺

Criticisms of mortgage brokers are largely centred on the basis that they may not have your best interests in heart. Some believe that their advice can be skewed to the direction of the highest commission. Or that they are affiliated to a particular service provider or have limited choices. Or better still that they have no idea of what they are doing. To ensure they are acting in your best interests, get those questions answered, ask for disclosure, do your own research and remember you don't need to go with the first one you see.

Obtaining pre-approval and its importance

Having a realistically idea of what you can actually afford is an important first step. Whether this starts by having a casual look using online calculators or actually consulting with a broker or lender, it is a good start and potential saver of disappointment later down the track.

When applying for pre-approval, you'll need to show:

- proof of deposit

- proof of income
- monthly expenses/ loans/ costs of living.

Meeting the basic requirements means you'll receive pre-approval. Benefits are:

1. Remains valid for three months.
2. Provides clear guidance on what you can afford.
3. Allows you to bid at auction with confidence.
4. Will prove to vendors that you're a motivated buyer and serious about taking action.
5. Saving time, as full approval can be achieved within one week, once pre-approval is in place.

Aspects to take into consideration when pre-approval is obtained:

It does not guarantee finance; it is only an indicator that the lender is "willing" to lend.

Lenders will approach pre-approval in different manners and assess different aspects. Therefore, different lenders could provide wildly different outcomes. It also won't help if you apply for pre-approval with multiple lenders. This will appear on your credit file and will only raise questions with the lender when you complete the full assessment.

The property will still be subject, in most cases, to valuation by the lender during the full assessment process.

If it expires, you will have to reapply.

Not all is lost if you are unable to achieve pre-approval. It might be that your application was a little premature. Maybe the credit rating score came back a little low, or not enough documentation or perhaps the Loan to Value Ratio was. If you don't secure pre-approval all is not lost. Reassess your financial situation and try and beef-up that deposit or minimise debts, and then try again.

How much to borrow

This is very much dependent on your ability to service the loan and the Loan to Value Ratio (LVR). The LVR aspect is particularly important as it is the amount of money borrowed against the value of the property (the bank's valuation assessment).

Now there are loan products available that will allow you to virtually borrow up to 100% of the property value. Strings are attached in these situations but it is not unheard of for people to secure finance at 95%, 90%, 85% etc. Now as a rule of thumb, 80% is the guideline for the LVR.

It is the guideline because having an LVR below 80% means that you will avoid Lenders

Mortgage Insurance (LMI). It can definitely be considered a way of getting into a property earlier but it will be another cost burden you will have to wear.

Most importantly, the following aspect must be remembered – LMI protects the lender not the borrower! This means that a lender will charge you additional money to insure the lender against the risk of the borrower defaulting on the loan. Tricky, huh? Lenders offer this product because it allows them to offer loans to a broader base of customers. This can be paid up-front or "capitalised" in that it is added to the total cost of the loan. Lenders will apply for the LMI on your behalf and GST will be added on top.

If you do default on the loan and the property is sold for a lower value than the initial loan, the insurer will make up the difference, payable to the bank. At this point in time, the insurer may ask you, as the borrower, to repay this sum directly to them!

Mortgage Protection Insurance (MPI) is available which in effect insures you in the event that something should prevent you from meeting your commitments (eg if you become ill, suffer an accident etc). Many variations are offered on this and it is something to consider, particularly if you have a family including dependants.

In summary, borrowing 80% or more will be a costly and potentially risky consideration. On the other hand, it can also be viewed as a necessary and worthwhile evil. However, to avoid paying LMI, save at least a 20% deposit, ask a close family member to be a guarantor (refer to pp. 88), use your First Home Buyers Grant as part of the deposit (refer to pp. 94) or study hard in school and become a professional as some occupations (such as doctors) will be exempt from LMI because of their future earning potential.

How banks will assess and the process they'll run

Here's a list of what you are actually required to bring:

1. ID – driver's license, passport, birth certificate, citizenship, Medicare card etc.

2. Your income – three months of pay slips. Bank statement showing salary deposits, tax returns and employment contracts. If you are self-employed, take one year's individual tax return and ATO assessment notice, or one year's tax return (P&L balance sheet).

3. PLUS any other income – eg shareholding statements, Centrelink statements confirming benefits etc

4. Proof of address, proof of savings and a list of any other assets that you have – shares, car/s, term deposits etc.

5. Liabilities – this is required so they can assess how much you can afford to borrow. So bring credit card statements, bank statements and other documentation that will confirm this.

6. Insurance – your current contents insurance and any income protection.

7. Property purchased/ construction contract. The bank needs to assess what you are actually buying. So bring:
   o Contract of sale
   o Council approved building plans
   o Priced building contract
   o Copy of the land transfer title
   o Proof of all other assets, super and personal insurance policies
   o Proof of property insurance

Now that you have your pieces of paper together, the bank will start their assessment.

Policies between lenders are going to differ but all of them will carefully assess you. The big ticket items you'll need to fulfil are:

1. Ability to repay – serviceability is a big factor in a lender's decision-making process. It is basically a judgement call by the bank on your ability to make the repayments and keep up a reasonable lifestyle without experiencing hardship,

particularly if interest rates should rise. Your income and outgoing expenses will all be considered as part of your ability to repay.

2. Deposit – how much are you actually bringing to the table and how does it affect the all important LVR? This aspect is important as your house will be used as "collateral" as in a hostage if you default. Therefore, what is it worth? And could the debt be recovered?

3. Credit history – have you missed repayments in the past? Have you defaulted on a loan or just collected one too many 'X' marks on your file. Unfortunately, the skeletons in the closet will catch up with you. Check out your credit report page at www.moneysmart.com.au to see how your credit scores are calculated.

4. Documentation – evidence of your earnings, proof a savings history and details on assets and liabilities will all be needed so the banks can feel confident that you meet the lending criteria.

If you are self-employed and unable to provide all the income information you could look into obtaining a low doc loan. This product allows you to obtain finance with simplified documentation.

Can I borrow with my significant other/ friend/ online mystery Nigerian man?

Absolutely, yes. Might suggest you look for an alternative if the online Nigerian is your partner but otherwise yes. You will be assessed together or as a group and the same conditions will apply. Your pooled deposit and joint income/s could be the factors that get you into a home quicker. For further details on this refer to pp. 160.

Will the bank take my rental history into account to assess my ability to repay a loan?

Yes some banks/ institutions will take a rental history into account as genuine savings. However, borrowers still require a minimum deposit level of 5% or more. This can come from a gift, windfall or the sale of an asset like a car. So if you have been a solid renter for 12 months or more and can show a stable history of repayments with regular contributions to savings, it will definitely provide the lender with confidence in your ability to service the loan.

Overall, it is a complicated process and different lenders will use different measures. However, having a stable career and demonstrating a history of savings will build real confidence with the lender. This could ultimately get your loan over the line.

How long will the application process take?

Obtaining pre-approval can be achieved within 48 hours. With pre-approval in place, it could take an additional week or so for unconditional finance to be achieved. If you start sourcing finance after you sign a contract, it will take a lot longer than you would expect or like. It is a nail-biting exercise. Generally, it will take 21 days, give or take, depending on how long it takes to get the documentation together and approved. Trust me; you sweat until you get that green light.

Borrowing options that are available

Minimum loan repayments will be calculated by working out what needs to be paid to reduce your loan to a zero over the life of the loan (usually 20 to 30 years). This will vary depending on interest rate movements and whether you make additional repayments. There are a lot of products and options available, all with different benefits and features. What's the right one? Well, it really just depends on your circumstances so consult with your lender or broker, and make your own assessment from there. And remember: the best loan for you doesn't necessary mean it will have the cheapest rate. Today, interest rates might not mean a lot to you but they soon will. These little puppies can have a big impact on the overall loan cost. A 1% movement upwards in rates could literally means $1000's in additional repayments. So let's look at interest rates in detail before discussing the loan options.

Interest Rates

Interest is essentially the cost incurred for borrowing and is set to achieve monetary policy outcomes. Monetary policy is basically a leaver pulled up or down to keep the economy in check.

The Reserve Bank of Australia (RBA) meets monthly, takes a number of economic measures into account and decides if the CASH RATE is right under current economic circumstances. This rate is the interest charged on overnight loans between the banks. RBA ➔ CASH RATE.

Now the cash rate is typically lower than the banks' official rate. Why? Because of their own costs for borrowing. That's called the cost of capital, but mainly because they also have some 'fat' on it and we all know banks are in the business of making money. This figure is actually the INTEREST RATE.

What's next ...?

Shop around and use a calculator to crunch the numbers. The cheapest rate doesn't automatically mean the cheapest loan. Check the fine print, check the fees and charges and do the sums.

This is where the Comparison Rate comes into account. This helps identify the true cost of the loan. This includes the interest rate, fees and charges reduced into a single percentage.

Principal – this is the ridiculously large figure that you've actually borrowed and will be paying back. A common loan type will be structured in a Principal + Interest (P&I) arrangement. Meaning repayments will cover interest costs and a deduction on the principal amount.

This is what is referred to as the Reducing Rate.

RBA ➔ CASH RATE ➔ INTEREST RATE ➔ COMPARISON RATE ➔ REDUCING RATE

Interest on your loan is calculated on a daily basis so the sooner you make the payments the better. Your type of loan and the bank itself will determine how often they'll allow payments. Generally though, always go for weekly or fortnightly repayments over monthly. Weekly/fortnightly will mean that you make an additional four weeks of payments per annum, saving big bucks over the life of the loan.

LOAN TYPES

Principal & Interest (P&I) and Interest Only

P&I is the most common type of lending product available. Each week/ fortnight or month your repayment will go towards reducing the

Principal and Interest accrued. Initially most of your repayments will get sucked up by interest charges but over time the amount owing decreases. This is why a loan can take 25 years to repay.

Taking out an Interest Only loan means that you will only ever be paying the interest and therefore the principal amount borrowed will not reduce. People who choose this type of loan are normally investors as the higher interest charges can be offset as a tax deduction. Also, the regular repayment amounts will be considerably less, compared to making P&I repayments.

Variable & Fixed Rate Loan

Variable essentially means that the rate will fluctuate up and down against the Cash Rate set by the RBA. A standard, variable loan can offer you flexibility and additional features. For example, my loan offers me a cheque book (surprisingly these things still exist) along with lump sum repayment options. Generally this type of loan is the basic, no bells-and-whistles type offering.

Fixed means locking it in! The best reason to choose a fixed rate loan is because repayments will stay the same for the agreed duration period. Essentially this provides you with certainty during the period in question. The disadvantages of fixed rates are that the lender may not let you make additional repayments.

Should the RBA drops the rate, then unfortunately you won't pick up that benefit. Also, these loans can be harder to get out of early, as penalties are likely to apply.

Guarantors

It's loan assistance, that's what it is. Someone, usually a close relative, could act as a Guarantor in order to provide additional security for the loan. The Guarantor effectively becomes the loan's guarantee in that, if you default, then the Guarantor becomes liable for the debt or a portion of the debt. Once the debt is paid down or the lender places more faith in your ability to service the debt (by having built up equity), the Guarantor can be released.

This works because the bank will effectively consider the equity in the Guarantor's asset, which is used as the additional security (collateral). The primary security is your home and the Guarantor is effectively acting as a back-up. Consider that your LVR is over 80%, if you could access a Guarantor, the equity in the additional property will help lower the LVR rate, allowing you to avoid LMI.

Usually, Guarantors are close family members like Mum or Dad, or perhaps a brother or a sister. Some banks will consider extended family members and other banks won't even consider a Guarantor at all. Some may request that the Guarantor is listed on the property title and, if you go down this route, it may mean that you'll lose your First Home Buyers Grant. It's a technicality, but having a person on the title that has bought property before could rule out your claim. If it does go pear-shaped, the implication is that the Guarantor will be held personally liable for the guarantee amount that they agreed to contractually. This could obviously have major ramifications for your future relationship with that person.

Combo Loans

These include the best elements of the variable and fixed rate loans. Under a combo loan, a portion becomes a variable loan and a portion is fixed.

Sounds nifty, doesn't it? 60/40 or 50/50 are more common but realistically it can be spilt any number of ways.

Honeymoon Rates

You've done the deed, signed your life away and are in bed with the bank. Because of this love affair is going so well the bank will drop their pants and give you a cheaper rate as a way of saying "I love you too." It's nice but like most relationships, the honeymoon period doesn't always last that long.

Line of Credit

It is like having a day-to-day transactional mortgage account. You deposit your monthly salary into the loan and use your credit card for day-to-day purchases. This card then gets transferred to your line of credit within the interest-free day period of the card. What this really means is that it allows you to simply draw down on repayments that are already made.

Mortgage Offset Account

This means that your loan account is linked to your regular savings account where your salary is deposited. While the cash sits in the account, it is offset against your loan therefore minimising the interest actually paid. The interest is calculated on the loan minus the balance of the account.

Shared Equity

This means someone else has a stake in the action. Banks can offer discounted rates on a proportion of the loan value in exchange for a share in the capital appreciation of the property value. Benefits are a lower rate and lower repayments which is pretty helpful when entering into the market. What's going against it is that someone else has a stake and a say on what goes on. In the past, this was offered by the WA Government under the First Start Shared Equity Home Loan Scheme. There is a lot of merit in this and it could be a great way of getting that initial step up the housing ladder.

There are many more products out there. As this is your first time however, keep it simple, shop around and make sure you understand the product and contract you are entering into.

Expenses

Apart from your deposit, there are a huge number of expenses that need to be taken into account. Some are one-offs; others will be ongoing on a weekly, monthly, quarterly or yearly cycle. Having an idea of what these will be is very useful for budgeting and influencing the initial loan value required. The table below is merely a guide on costs associated with loans. Depending on where you live, how much you borrow and the type of loan or lender will influence these costs as they are by no means fixed.

Bank Fees and Charges

Deposit – a one off expense	10% of asking price.
Lending Fees	**Approximate Cost**
Loan application fee – generally includes settlement and search fees	$600
Valuation fee – major lenders will include this in the application	$0 to $250
Monthly loan service fee	$0 - $10

Mortgage Protection Insurance (MPI) – will depend on how much you borrow.	$1500 to $3000+
Lender Mortgage Insurance (LMI) – a one-off expense	Will vary on the LVR and the size of the loan. They can be from 0.5% to 5% of the loan amount.

Government Costs

Government Fees	Approximate Costs – based on a purchase price of $550,000 for an existing property as your principal residence
Transfer fee	$100 to $4,000
Stamp duty - will vary from state to state. What is Stamp Duty Anyway? It is a tax levied by the state for the transfer of property. The duty will vary depending on what you buy and each state will have different variances. Working out how much you'll need can get confusing because of differences, concessions, and different rates for land and also mortgage duty.	QLD - $10,600 NSW - $20,240 VIC - $12,485 ACT - $18,300 SA - $24,080 NT - $27,225 TAS - $20,372 WA - $20,140

Generally the cheaper the property, the less duty you'll pay. Also some states provide a concession for first home buyers. Check with your Office of State Revenue to see what you are eligible for.	
Mortgage registration – normally collected by the lender	$100 · $200

Other Costs

OTHER COSTS	APPROXIMATE COSTS
Conveyancing fee	$500 to $2000
Search fee	$200 to $400
Sundries/ settlement	$100
Building report	$500
Pest inspection	$300 to $500
Insurance	$1000 (depends on location, value etc.)
Moving	$1000
Decking out the new pad	The sky is the limit
Connecting utilities – a one off fee	Water, gas, electricity, internet, cable TV
Utilities monthly	$50 to $100
Rates quarterly	$350 · $600
Body corporate fee	$300 · $3000+
Mortgage account keeping fees	Loans might be subject to the yearly fee

To download a free home loan and general expenses check-list please refer to the www.thebuyersguide.com.au

Now you know the true cost of your purchase.

Concessions, Taxes and Government Charges

Entitlements on offer relate to the First Home Buyers Grant (FHBG) and in some States/ Territories concessions for Stamp Duty are offered. Check your eligibility at www.firsthome.gov.au along with the latest updates that apply to your State/ Territory.

When Australia introduced the GST, the government thought they would help chip in for first home buyers. In actual fact, this was really one of the major catalysts for the start of the housing boom of the early 2000's. Since its introduction, the FHBG scheme has morphed and changed and it now varies from state to state.

To claim your grant, you'll need:

1. To be an Australian citizen/ or hold Permanent Residency
2. Live in the property for at least 12 months
3. Only claim the grant once and meet the conditions of purchase value.

The Grant value will vary from state to state but at present it looks something like this:

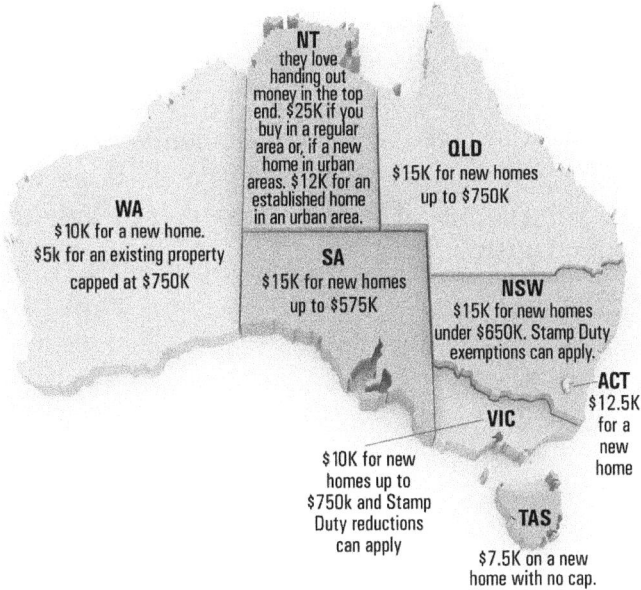

NT
they love handing out money in the top end. $25K if you buy in a regular area or, if a new home in urban areas. $12K for an established home in an urban area.

QLD
$15K for new homes up to $750K

WA
$10K for a new home. $5k for an existing property capped at $750K

SA
$15K for new homes up to $575K

NSW
$15K for new homes under $650K. Stamp Duty exemptions can apply.

ACT
$12.5K for a new home

VIC
$10K for new homes up to $750k and Stamp Duty reductions can apply

TAS
$7.5K on a new home with no cap.

To stay up to date, please refer to your State's relevant Office of State Revenue. These websites are:

ACT – www.revenue.act.gov.au

NSW – www.osr.nsw.gov.au

NT – www.treasury.nt.gov.au

QLD – www.greatstartgrant.osr.qld.gov.au

SA – www.revenuesa.sa.gov.au

TAS – www.sro.tas.gov.au

VIC – www.sro.vic.gov.au

WA – www.finance.wa.gov.au

Now two options exist across all states when you apply for the FHBG:

1. Lodge application through an approved agent, being a bank or a broker
2. Download application form, complete it and lodge it yourself. Remember to show evidence all your paperwork, ID, as well as copies of the sales contract or building contract.

Stamp Duty

Stamp duty is a tax levied on your property purchase. It is likely to be the single biggest expense incurred outside of the purchase price. Like the FHBG, Stamp Duty is levied by the states/ territories and each area has a different levy. Referring to the above websites is a good source of information but generally speaking the amount will be based on the value of the property and payable in 30 days of purchase.

KEY CHAPTER POINTS

1. Mortgage products can be obtained directly from banking institutions or sourced through a third party such as a mortgage broker. Carefully assess your options and work with the one that feels right for you.

2. Be organised, gather all the relevant documents and see your bank or broker and work towards achieving pre-approval. This is very important as it will provide you with an understanding of what you can afford. Reminder => it does not guarantee finance but merely indicates the bank's willingness to lend.

3. The Loan to Value Ratio (LVR) is the percentage of the asset value against the size of the loan. The asset value and deposit is taken into consideration. Basically the more you borrow, the 'riskier' you are to the bank. Therefore, they want a buffer.

4. The bank's assessment of you will include your ability to repay, the deposit size, current history, and the documentation you can present. Essentially, they want to see the paperwork to determine you are a good financial citizen who can meet and repay your debts.

5. Guarantors can help you get the loan approval over the line.

6. There is a stack of mortgage products on the market. The industry is competitive so shop around and choose the one that is best for you.

7. Lenders Mortgage Insurance (LMI) – is a burden cost that will protect the lender if you default on the loan. Basically, it is an insurance policy you pay on behalf of the bank to insure them if you default. It the LVR is above 80%, LMI will likely be required.

8. Mortgage Protection Insurance (MPI) – insures you in the event should something happen that prevents you from making payments.

9. Claim your first home buyers grant and any other additional incentives that you may be entitled to.

10. Borrowing with another individual is totally acceptable and both/ all parties will be assessed.

11. Some lenders will take your rental history into account and can view it as savings.

12. Interest rates are very important. They fluctuate up and down, and even small moves up can have a big impact on the household budget.

13. RBA ➔ CASH RATE ➔ INTEREST RATE ➔ COMPARISON RATE ➔ REDUCING RATE

14. There are numerous home loan products available. Assess each on their merits and chose the one that is best for you. This doesn't necessarily mean the cheapest one.

15. Dozens of additional expenses will creep into the process. Charges will be associated with actual purchase, associated services and others relating to securing finance. Amounts will vary depending on the provider and the actual property amount purchased.

16. Concessions are available in some states for Stamp Duty. First Home Buyer Grants can also be obtained although conditions apply. Try to get every cent you are entitled to and stay abreast of the latest changes from your Office of State Revenue.

SOURCING AND
BUYING PROPERTY

Facebook might just get a demotion as the most viewed website as more and more people are viewing real estate web listings. It can be difficult to decide where to start. Naturally, you would start with www.thebuyersguide.com.au and perhaps, after that, just get talking. Speak to family, friends and colleagues about their experiences and most importantly seek some professional advice. Decide on your preferences in particular locations and commence studying your subject: this being, researching the suburb of your choice and making a decision on other locational aspects that are important to you. Broaden your net to include surrounding suburbs and start the practical element by attending as many open houses that align to your requirements as possible. Some suggest visiting up to 100 open houses to get a true appreciation of where the market is. There are a lot of quality online sources and a good first place to commence is registering with www.realestate.com.au and www.domain.com.au and selecting your preferences for email alerts.

So the phone and laptop will get a good workout and the car will run up some kms on a Saturday doing the open house runs but the day will come... that beautiful property that you imagined will appear, you'll go weak at the knees and try and hold back the excitement when your offer is accepted. A lot of hard work was required to get to this point so enjoy the moment. To help this process a little, we will cover off what to expect from the purchase and negotiation process to secure a satisfying outcome.

Research

- How to source
- What resources are available?
- Real estate agents
- Open houses
- Pricing
- Frustration
- Buyer's agents

How to source

It is an audacious task and much like any project, it's about planning. If you are anything like me, when you were at school, your best projects were normally a copy of someone else's work or a slight creative alternative. So by that rationale, if people have been successful or have already secured the property that you've been looking for, why wouldn't you follow their approach?

Let's look at how others may have approached this "project":

1. Commence with historical data to find recent sale prices for similar properties in similar locations for the past 12 months. Some good websites to look at include

realestate.com.au/ domain.com.au/ onthehouse .com.au/ rpdata.com.au which will have records of sale prices results. These sources are sometimes available for free but quite often a charge is involved. The Australian Bureau of Statistics (ABS) and Local Council websites can also be good sources of information relating to local demographics.

2. Map out where the amenities are in your area. A great reference site for this task is walkscore.com.au which will locate shops, places of interest, public transport, hospitals etc. that are within walking distance of your place. A good Walkscore is all important.

3. Infrastructure and suburban planning – check with the local council planning committees and city planning schemes. What's in store for your suburb over the next ten years? It's important to know because you wouldn't want to lose your footpath to road widening or even your whole house if a new freeway or train line that will be built close by.

4. Aspect – what is the property's vista? Where will the sun hit in the early morning and late afternoon? (Something quite simple but quite annoying when you're waking up to the sun in your eyes every day at 5am).

5. Entitlements - get the best bang for your

buck. Get every cent you're entitled to (refer to pp. 88). Be sure you understand the terms and conditions of entitlements and concessions like the FHBG and Stamp Duty concessions to maximise every dollar you can get.

6. Costs – fees, charges and miscellaneous items you may not have even considered (refer to pp. 91) all need to be accounted for. They quickly add up and there a plenty of sneaky extras. It is very worthwhile to be on the front foot of what money is actually leaving your pocket.

Watching and anticipating the right market entry points for you will probably dictate your long-term game. Be mindful that falling home prices could mean that there are broader issues in the economy; lower rates could also start heating-up the market. But falling prices and a general lack of confidence can usually mean that bargains are to be had. Watch for the latest news, follow demand and supply and target the in-demand areas in a slow market and you could snag a real winner.

There isn't a need to tackle all of the above all at once but pick the ones that are of immediate importance for you and tailor the research to the specific property that you find. Informed decisions will ensure a solid buy.

What resources are available?

Obviously the first choice would be the www.thebuyersguide.com.au but outside of this you can also refer to:

- www.moneysmart.gov.au
- www.firsthome.gov.au
- www.yourhome.gov.au
- www.rpdata.com.au
- www.onthehouse.com.au
- www.walkscore.com.au
- www.residex.com.au
- www.realestate.com.au
- www.domain.com.au
- www.reia.asn.au
- www.api.org.aue
- www.openagent.com.au*
- www.homepriceguide.com.au*

Charges apply for sourcing sales and price data.

Every State has an Office of State Revenue and these are also excellent sources of relevant information regarding local Stamp Duty and First Home Buyers Grants.

ACT – www.revenue.act.gov.au

NSW – www.osr.nsw.gov.au

NT – www.treasury.nt.gov.au

QLD – www.greatstartgrant.osr.qld.gov.au

SA – www.revenuesa.sa.gov.au

TAS – www.sro.tas.gov.au

VIC – www.sro.vic.gov.au

WA – www.finance.wa.gov.au

There are literally 1000's of sites with relevant information, and some also contain opinions and get-rich-quick schemes. Most, you will notice, will target investors and apart from www.thebuyersguide.com.au don't specifically cater for First Home Buyers. Don't discount them. There is excellent FREE information available but be wary of services asking for money up-front. The information could be great but in most cases it's generic and offers a hook to buy the next edition. Also, with a little Googling and some creativity, you can often find the same information for free.

Real estate agents

During your research you'll be attending open houses, looking at real estate windows, spending a lot of time online and you will have a fair amount of contact with real estate agents. So, are they friends or foes? Neither really, they are just the conduit between the vendor and the buyer. The vendor is paying a fee for service so the real estate agents are working for their client's best interests and are doing so contractually. They are just doing their job which means getting the best price for the vendor. While they are working for the vendor you are the one with the money so you have considerable influence yourself.

In short, treat agents how you wish to be treated. When you find the ideal place (and it will happen), you don't want the agent to be the one you've been stalking or got on the wrong side of at last week's open house.

Seek out the reputable players. You'll tend to find that agents will specialise in a particular area. Target the ones that are most active and get to know them and they may even give you a "heads up" on future listings.

So how do you identify a good agent?

- Good communication skills, particularly in a time-sensitive market
- Good listener. If they talk too much, keep walking
- Their clients' needs are their top priority
- Good negotiators.
- They show respect.

Respect and consideration go both ways:

- Don't be a control freak. Let them do their job.
- Book a time and stick to it. People are busy and therefore not turning up to a

scheduled appointment without notice is rude.

- Be honest. Otherwise you are just wasting your time and theirs.

Use the real estate agent for researching and obtaining additional information. The place you've just inspected may not suit but that doesn't necessarily mean that the agent doesn't have a new suitable listing coming up next week. Most people when they attend an open house prefer to keep contact with the agent to a minimum. A wasted opportunity in my opinion. If you like the property or are open to just having a chat, put these questions into your holster:

- Why is the vendor selling?
- How long has it been on the market?
- Will they negotiate on the price?
- How soon do they want to move out?
- Who set the property price?
- What do you think it will sell for?
- What does the property come with? Any additional furniture or appliances included?
- What else do you have at this price?
- What are the property defects?
- Any other serious offers?
- Where do I need to be at in order to buy this property today?!!!

If you are serious about buying, I'm sure that by the time the process is complete, you will have a few stories to share. It's all part of the learning experience. Be patient, don't waste time with unrealistic expectations and get to know your local market because when the right place comes up, you'll be able to instinctively pounce.

Open houses

You've cleared the decks and you are going house shopping Saturday morning. Feel good? Tie your shoes tight, grab your "shopping list" and tackle the first open house head on.

You've pulled up, parked, and then realised, shit, there are other people here as well, lots of people actually. Anyway, forget them, get your strut on, sign the book and start scoping the joint. Not for things to pinch, but to determine if the place will actually stack up. While you're strutting, check out these things:

- Water stains/ corrosions/ smells/ dampness/ mould… moisture is a killer so avoid it.
- Cabinets in wet areas, have a quick peep.
- Sagging ceilings or cracks in the walls could indicate structural defects.
- Roof… asbestos, rusty gutters or down pipes… might be worth avoiding.
- Check room sizes and importantly layout.

- Turn the taps on – is there good water pressure?
- What is the condition of the garden? Fencing, privacy and security... how do they stack up?
- What do the exterior walls look like?
- How many neighbours are there? What is the condition of their property like?

There are many more conditions to look at and it is unrealistic to uncover all of them in the first 10-15 minute inspection. If you like the property, book a second viewing and follow up with a building and pest inspection for additional assurance. For a Home Inspection Checklist refer to www.thebuyersguide.com.au

Now the house/ apartment/ townhouse may look ugly but it could have the potential to be a bargain. So take a look at the whole picture because sometimes you'll find a diamond in the rough.

Speak with the agent and ask these questions:

- Are they aware of any property defects?
- How active is the body corporate if you are looking at a unit etc?
- Is any major maintenance or project work planned?
- Have any previous offers been submitted?
- If yes, why did they get rejected?

111

- Have any building/ pest inspections being completed already?

Pricing

The biggest deciding factor generally boils down to price. Determining the sale price can be formulated by looking at:

- Recent sale prices
- Market trends
- Comparisons to new listing in your local market
- Days on the market and whether these sales have been above or below trend.

As we discussed before the property market, over any period of time, will fluctuate like the weather. No matter the weather forecast at the time it will either favour The Buyers or The Sellers. Signals that may indicate that it is a buyers market:

- Long periods of being "for sale"
- Lower housing prices
- Property listed with multiple agents
- Agents themselves are responsive and regularly calling for feedback/ updates
- Volume of property or "stock" increases
- Low numbers of visitors numbers at open houses.

112

The opposite of these factors tends to take place when it is a sellers' market: prices are higher, property transactions turn over quickly and there is a general sense of hype.

When you commence your search, you quickly realise that getting a clear-cut price will be next to impossible. Instead you will encounter "Prices Ranges" or "Offers Above" or "Bidding From," frustrating when you only want to know an actual price. It could be argued that these statements are misleading but it is standard practice. No-one wants to show their full hand. The only way to know a price is to have done your research. Get to know the market, go to auctions, visit open houses, get to know the competition (you'll likely see the same people each Saturday; it can be weird). The more you know the market, with similar house price sales, the better as this will place you in a position of strength when offering to buy or when negotiating the sales contract. Another method, although not foolproof is to use the guideline prices on property search engines. No matter the listing an agent will be required to submit a price in order for the property to become searchable in the listings. For example, you can get a guestimate by looking with your price range say $450,000 to $500,000, find a place you like and then reset the price range to $450,000 to $475,000. Does the property still come up in the search? If so, keep tweaking and see what results you can get. Not 100% accurate but, like I said, it can give you a reasonable indication.

Price ranges or guidelines are used so agents can create a sense of urgency or scarcity. It is a tactic to play on the emotions to help influence the price. Having a lot of people at an open house who are expressing interest increases the sense of competition. Not having a set price plays to all those factors. The guideline is merely a guideline. The agent is likely to know the market. But the vendor usually has a heightened sense of what the property is worth because of their own emotional attachment. By that rationale, the real price is probably somewhere in the middle.

One way to overcome price uncertainty is to be certain with your own finances. By having pre-approval, you'll truly know what you can afford and back it up with a rock solid budget. Secondly, is to have done your research. Know what has sold and when. Educate yourself with what has been going on and make an informed decision. If it's not right for you, just keep walking. There are plenty of other houses out there. All you need is a little patience.

The true price of a property is what someone is actually prepared to pay for it at that point in time. Uncertainty is likely to always be a factor so the best thing to achieve is to be happy with the end result you achieve. If you still have doubts, maybe also consider getting an independent valuation. Make this a contractual clause – "subject to valuation" which could be a great negotiating tool.

Frustrations

The journey for a first home buyer is not an easy one. It will be littered with frustrations and challenges and the only way to prepare is to educate yourself and be on the front foot. So to pre-empt the factors that will get on your nerves here is a convenient list:

1. Spending your Saturdays going from one property to the next, seeing some properties that may be run down and that you don't want to live in and maybe can't even afford.

2. The speed of which some places will sell, along with obtaining multiple offers.

3. The competition of other first home buyers and cashed up baby boomers buying investments under their self-managed super fund, along with foreign investors snapping up properties will be frustrating.

4. Large proportion of properties that go to auction.

5. Nobody is ever prepared to give you a realistic price.

6. Coming to terms with your expectations and the actual reality.

7. How long and difficult it can be to save a deposit.

8. Uncertainty in the process.

9. Commitment of a debt partnership (home loan) for 25-30 years.

10. Compromising with your partner on what you both want.

It's normal to feel frustrated throughout such a process, but just maintain a calm state because what will be will be. Plus, you will never buy if you stay hiding under your doona. You need to be out there, and you need to be making relationships. If there is one thing I've learnt through my own experiences is that people do business with people they like. Have fun with the process, crack a joke with the agent, and chat to the other buyers. Seeing the lighter side of it all will alleviate some of the stress.

And, mostly importantly, educate yourself and become 'hip' about what to expect.

Buyer's agents

Buyers' agents are slowly starting to come into vogue because of their expertise in sourcing and negotiating the property purchase on your behalf. They can be a worthy consideration because it's like having a hired gun doing the job for you. Think of them as a coach. They should educate, challenge and point you in the right direction for the best outcome for both of you.

You could use a Buyer's Agent to bid at the auction on your behalf. They could take a brief, search, find and negotiate the purchase on your behalf. They can charge a flat fee or a percentage of the purchase price.

The benefits for you are access to their networks and their expertise and hopefully skills as negotiators. They can also save you time. In some cases, their individual expertise could be of significant value, saving you the legwork as well. This could be a particularly useful service if you are purchasing in a different state or region. Go with a Buyer's Agent who is local to the area, on the basis of a home-ground advantage. The critical success factor is to be particularly clear about your expectations; otherwise you may be disappointed with the search results they produce.

Engaging with a Buyer's Agent requires due diligence. Go for a fee structure that is performance/ outcome based and do background checks. Make sure they are licensed, and consider taking references as well. Always ensure they are independent and not affiliated with particular agents. Remember they aren't doing this for free so don't forget to include their costs into the purchase price.

If the Buyer's Agent has his or her finger on the pulse and really knows the market, and also procures the property for you, the whole relationship could really work to your advantage.

For recent first home buyer listings in your area check out the www.buyersguide.com.au

Purchase

Simply put, there are only two things that you should consider when purchasing:

1. Buy what you can afford
2. Buy what feels right for you.

OK, so that wasn't earth shattering stuff but they are the only things you really need to know.

Point one is self-explanatory, albeit that it's tempting to sign up for more than you can afford and say statements like, "honey, we'll make it work!" It's understandable to be faced with such a temptation, but circumstances change, interest rates fluctuate, life serves up lemons and, disappointingly, bills will always continue to come in. What if you lost your job? Can you really afford to support yourself for a few months? Be smart and stay within your means. Sometimes the juice just isn't worth the squeeze.

When you start discussing your motivation to buy with others, you'll start running into opinions, including opinions on what you should buy and where. This is where the second point above comes in because ultimately this property

first home
THE BUYERS GUIDE

is going to be yours, that is, the place where you'll get horizontal at night and hide when the world seems that little bit too scary. So it's important to buy what feels right for you on a variety of levels. Now that could be a one bed-apartment located close to the city or a two acre block that is an hour away from work. Really, it doesn't matter, as long as it feels right for you.

To walk you through the process of purchasing we'll look into the following:

1. House vs. apartment
2. Private treaty sales
3. Auctions
4. Negotiation
5. Pre-cautionary measures.

House vs. apartment

Guess we should revert back to the earlier comment – Buy what feels right for you. In deciding that, factors such as lifestyle, forward planning, financial implications and potential for growth all come into play. By taking these factors into account either house or apartment could be the right option because of the number of different variables involved – truly it just depends. After lifestyle and forward planning requirements, the clincher is for potential capital growth.

The age-old argument between the two is that apartments represent value-for-money because they have a lower price entry point. Alternatively, freestanding houses have land around them which appreciates in value when the dwelling house/ unit block depreciates. While this is a fair statement to a certain extent, demographics and society have changed and a lot of people choose proximity to the city centre as a more appealing aspect.

Hypothetically, if you are pre-approved to buy a $500k property, think about what's more important in these factors:

FACTORS	APARTMENT	HOUSE
Lifestyle	*Proximity and location to city/ major urban area *Requirement to abide by the by-laws *May have additional facilities like social/ break out areas, gyms, sauna and pool.	*Additional room to move but is potentially a further distance away from urban hubs *Can renovate as you wish to council regulations.
Forward planning	Think about your current and future lifestyle needs particularly if you wish to start a family. Ongoing costs can be higher in a house as everything is the owner's responsibility compared to a shared cost in a building. With an apartment, you'll have responsibility for upkeep and will require additional contributions for building maintenance, insurance and future work. Your forward planning may also take into consideration whether you intend to keep	

	the property as an investment or sell it. Again, different factors will need to be considered in each option.
Financial implications	The process of securing a loan in either arrangement will be exactly the same. The additional implications will be on the future ongoing costs basis which you should cover off in your forward planning.
Growth	As demand for inner-city living increases, then the land that these properties sit on becomes increasingly valuable. Apartment developments are more likely to spring up in inner-city areas and owning one of the apartments is an ownership in the shared rising value of the land. But not all things are created equal so poorly located or designed apartments may miss out on any increases in value. So too do complexes that have 100's of units on the one block because of the smaller proposition of land holdings you'll individually own.

If you are starting your search take both options into consideration. Do inspections across all property types whether they be apartments, townhouses, duplexes and/ or detached houses. The more you see the more in tune you'll become with what you actually want. You may decide that after looking at apartments for several weeks that they are simply too small for your liking. Also, after doing several trial runs in peak hour traffic, the commuting grind may be too stressful to handle on a daily basis. A change in preference may appear before you, but you won't come to realise this until after you start getting amongst it.

Private treaty sale

This is generally the most common way in which a property is purchased. Private treaty is where you negotiate the purchase of a property, including the price directly with the vendor/ real estate agent. The benefit of private treaty sales are the flexibility they offer the vendor the opportunity to negotiate and they will have 'subject to' clauses which refer to finance approval and building and pest inspections. There will also be a 'cooling off' period. To understand the contractual implications under a Private treaty sale, refer to (pp. 137).

Auctions

Going once... Going twice... Going three times... no final offers... SOLD! We all know the words but in actual fact an auction is quite different in that it is a 'cash' purchase and you are generally entering an Unconditional Contract once the hammer falls. A deposit of around 10% of agreed purchase price is generally payable. This is a great reason why real estate agents will go to auction as it pushes people to commit on the day.

Auctions really come into vogue during a sellers' market. Auctions play on people's emotions but in a concentrated manner. Vendors hope that this emotional play will push up the end result and also achieve an unconditional contract.

What is the auction process?

Before auction day, if there is interest in the property complete building/ pest inspections and, if required by your state, register as a bidder. Registering is required in some states to eliminate "dummy bidding."

On the day of the auction, the Auctioneer/ Agent will have agreed on a 'Reserve Price' with the vendor. Once this price is achieved, the property is technically "on the market" and will sell on the fall of the hammer. Before the bidding commences, the Auctioneer will announce/ detail information relating to the specific state laws and rules that apply. These rules vary from region to region so discuss this with the Agent beforehand.

The auction will then commence for an 'Opening Bid' where the Auctioneer will ask for someone to start off proceedings. Sometimes, the Auctioneer may call it themselves and indicate they are taking bids in $5k/ $10k/ $20k increments. Now you can bid in any amount outside of the specified range but it is up to Auctioneer's discretion whether it is accepted as you might try and put in a low bid when plenty of other bidders are wanting to keep the momentum going.

This is where things get tricky in an auction process because of the dynamics of others competing all at once. If the momentum completely stalls and bidding is below the reserve price, the Auctioneer can pause the auction to speak to the vendor. The Auctioneer may ask for the vendor to consider a lower price or to make a "vendor's bid." With a vendor's bid, the Auctioneer can come back and indicate that the vendor has made a bid of $X and that they'll take increments of $X. Generally this is an indication that the auction isn't going well for the vendor so it will either "pass in" meaning that is hasn't achieved the desired price and the auction has completed. Alternatively, if the Auctioneer announces that it is "on the market", it will be closed on the fall of the hammer to the highest bidder.

If the property is "passed in" and doesn't sell, usually the vendor will try to negotiate with the highest bidder on the day to close out a deal.

What to be aware of

1. An immediate deposit (usually 10% of purchase price) is required after the auction. The balance will be paid upon settlement.

2. There is no cooling-off period.

3. Building and pest inspections will need to be completed prior to the auction and the contract will not be subject to these clauses.

4. Your finance will need to be approved prior to committing to the contract as it is a cash sale.

A word about deposit bonds - these are cost-effective ways to cover the deposit on your purchase when you cannot immediately access the cash; however you will need to have your finance approved. The bond will be equal value to the deposit. The bond can be viewed as an insurance policy in that money doesn't actually exchange hands and the funds will be paid in full at settlement. Basically the deposit bond is offered as a fallback measure in that, if you forfeit the contract, the vendor can recoup the deposit through insurance. If using or thinking of using this method, seek professional legal advice as there are catches and in some purchasing arrangements they won't be accepted.

Here are a couple of tips for the auction day:

- Bid with confidence.

- Bid in unusual numbers. People will look at you funny and that's because it's off putting; just another way of playing the game.

- Don't get caught up in the hype. Don't let the agent pressure you and get in your face. There is a thing called 'Personal Space'; make sure it's respected.

125

- Don't set your limit on a round figure because it may mean missing out by a marginal amount. Say you set your price at $500k but it sells for $507k; it's likely you'll be a little miffed if that happens. However, stay within your budget.

Get some practice too, go to a few auctions to watch and observe; give it a bit of a test run. Get to know the whole process and on the day stick to your budget, have your admin sorted, be registered to bid, bring the deposit and bring a friend so you can squeeze their hand throughout the process or they can rein in your enthusiasm if you get too carried away and start wanting to bid beyond your limit. Good luck!

Negotiation

Numerous books have been written on the art of negotiation so let's try and give it some justice with a few tips to consider.

Now in a Private Treaty arrangement it will be likely that you'll have had a bit of interaction with the agent and, being human, they'll have preconceived ideas. The vendor will have a price they need or want and they add in some 'fat'. Imagine that 'fat' to be 20%. And you're probably thinking that it is worth 20% less, so realistically it's going to be somewhere in between.

With the first offer, put it in writing. Legally agents are required to take written offers to the vendor. Check out www.thebuyersguide.com.au for a free template on how the letter could look. Now a low verbal offer may make an agent nervous particularly if they've over-promised the vendor. Even better staple a cheque with your deposit to your letter of offer. No need to worry as it will only be cashed when the offer is accepted. With a written offer and a deposit in hand: first, it will show how serious you are; and second, it speaks volumes to the vendor subconsciously as they will feel that they're close to securing a deal. Sure there might be some back-and-forth, to-ing and fro-ing but it is a great way of getting them to the table even if the offer is lower than their guideline price, within reason. When you are going backwards and forwards on price, never reveal your walk away price as they will attempt to get as close as possible to that outcome.

Negotiation may not always be about price! If you have an idea of the vendor's motivations, great! If not, maybe just ask the agent, as the highest price may not always be the real sweetener. Maybe you could do a quickie sale. If you're pre-approved and they want out, this could be the perfect sweetener for them. Or perhaps you could be willing to have a clause or two to speed up the deal. Alternatively, the vendor may need more time to pack up and arrange their next move (eg to a retirement village). In such a case, consider a longer settlement period than normal (eg 60 days instead of 30). Do whatever you feel will get it over the line, and always seek professional advice prior to committing to, or even omitting any, contractual terms.

Also, instead of negotiating on price, consider looking at other factors... ask for furniture to be included into the contract. Nice lounge setting, telly, outdoor setting – items that people could well be prepared to give you, if it means closing the deal.

Negotiation is highly dependent of the state of the market. In a buyers' market, you could throw a lowball offer and get it over the line. In a sellers' market, you may have to pay above the asking price. However, if the house/ flat ticks all the boxes, just give it a red-hot go. But if not, there are a lot of other 'perfect' (sometimes even more perfect) places out there.

Pre-cautionary measures

Given that you are making one of the biggest investments of your life, it is a good idea to play it safe to achieve the best outcome. Price will generally always be the biggest factor and you don't want to be overpaying. To ensure that this won't happen, seek out an independent valuation beforehand.

Use a good conveyancer – you want to ensure that the property is unencumbered and that you are purchasing a property with a clean title. This prevents hidden surprises popping up down the track. Conveyancing will also uncover easements and boundary lines. It is important to ensure what you are perceived to be buying is, in fact, what you're actually getting.

And the three simple factors that could get you unstuck are:

1. Being too emotionally invested – agents and vendors can smell desperation. You fallen in love and want to shout it from the rooftops. If you start doing this, you'll also see the dollar signs rolling in the real estate agent's eyes.

2. Not knowing the market – do your research, have knowledge of previous comparable prices and do this prior to making an offer.

3. Not being ready and able – being a false starter is never good. Time and money can be lost into the abyss. Be pre-approved for finance, complete the necessary inspections, use a conveyancer and be prepared to go through the slog of negotiation, stress and worry that can be generated from the process until it is finalised.

The dream is out there for everyone. Disappointingly, the potential to buy the dream requires the right brief, having your finances together, and knowing what you can afford. Be prepared to be patient and then you will find the right home.

Patience through this phase will pay big dividends, particularly to your stress levels. Do your due diligence and if it feels right, go for it. If it doesn't, for whatever reason, keep walking.

KEY CHAPTER POINTS:

Buy what you feel is right for you and your budget

1. Commence your research by looking at historical data on sales prices and market activity for your target region/ location. Find out what amenities are available. A good tool is www.walkscore.com.au

2. Future planning – what's the development proposed for in 5 – 10 years' time? What will your suburb look like in the future? Refer to City Plans through the council.

3. If you are entitled to a Grant or can receive a concession, get it! The extra money will be helpful as costs have a funny way of quickly adding up.

4. There are literally hundreds of web resources available for FREE. www.thebuyersguide.com.au is also a dedicated authority for first home buyers.

5. Real estate agents are just the conduit between you and the vendor. A key aspect in your relationship with them is to ask questions and use their knowledge as an additional research tool.

6. Communication and mutual respect are keys to forming good relationships with Real Estate Agents.

7. Vet a property through open houses. Don't be shy, have a sticky beak and open a cupboard or two. If you feel confident that it is up to scratch get a building/ pest inspection completed prior to closing the deal.

8. Pricing and obtaining a true indication of what a vendor wants can be frustrating. Do your research and understand where the market is at. The true value of a property is what someone is willing to pay for it.

9. Buyers' agents can be used as a gun for hire. They can source and negotiate the sale on your behalf. Consider them as a coach and you'll get the best out of them because you are also learning and are challenging yourself to perform and achieve the desired end result = home ownership.

10. Stick with what your budget is and buy a home that feels right for you.

11. Buying what feels right for you will steer you down the track of a home or an apartment. Both are fine options but lifestyle, forward planning, financial implications and growth potential all need to be taken into consideration prior to buying.

12. Private treaty sale is the most common type of transaction. It is where you negotiate the purchase either directly with the vendor or real estate agent.

13. Auctions are a cash purchase and on the fall of the hammer you enter into an unconditional contract. This means you must have your finances in place, inspections must be completed prior to the auction, and there will be no cooling-off period.

14. Auctions are used to create urgency, competition and pushes buyers to commit on a "cash" basis.

15. Sharpen your skills and be bold to achieve the best price. Be confident and chance your hand when it comes to negotiating, as you never know what the outcome could be. Also, negotiating doesn't have to always be about price. Perhaps a speedy deal or a couch/ fridge thrown in could be enough to get it over the line.

16. Consider getting an independent valuation, use a conveyancer/ solicitor and source professional advice wherever you feel is necessary or you feel unsure.

SORTING OUT THE RULES OF ENGAGEMENT AND GETTING THE "ADMIN" RIGHT

Administratively, the process of buying a home and securing finance is according to my wife... intensive, stressful, daunting and traumatic. The last 'adjective' actually made me laugh out loud. It can be all of these things but is never usually that bad. The contract is king though and it is absolutely imperative you understand the document prior to putting your autograph anywhere. Depending on where you live, different criteria will apply but in all cases a contract requires an agreement by both parties on the offer and acceptance. While you can be put off by the length and complex terminology, which triggers a realization of the importance of the document, you should be aware that there avenues to 'flex' or renege on the contract should something not sit completely right. On the flipside the seller has very few contingencies to leverage, should they wish to get out of the contract which is comforting to know to a certain extent.

Understanding the contract of sale

1. Private treaty
2. Auction
3. Off the plan

This is the Terms and Conditions (T&Cs). The T&Cs are long and have lots of "sign here" stickers. These are generally considered as the identifying marks. Other distinguishing factors include ambiguous terms and they have also been used as sleeping aids (*yawn*). Boring, yes, but it's definitely really important, so try to stick with it.

Private treaty sale

Buying through an agent or private seller means that you will be entering into a Private Treaty Sale. The contract is legally binding once it is signed by both parties and ensures the property is not sold to another higher bidder. Prior to signing, arrange for your solicitor/ conveyancer to advise you on the legal process and to look through the contract you wish to sign. Once signed, you are entering into a "Treaty" and a holding deposit will be payable.

This deposit is put down in good faith. Technically you only need to put down $1 however; agents and vendors will question your intentions should you do so. Real estate agents will typically take their commission from the deposit hence why they would motivate you to provide additional funds. This deposit will usually be held in a trust account by the real estate agent. Normally, 5% should suffice however use judgement in each scenario. Sometimes, say where the purchase price is around the $550K mark, you could be asked for a deposit of $2K upon making your offer, followed by an additional $25K when the contract becomes unconditional (eg after the building and pest inspection is OK and you have secured your finance, say, within 14 days).

To bulletproof your process make sure you check out www.thebuyersguide.com.au

Now the essence of this contract is a checklist which covers off:

1. Address and physical dimensions of the property

2. Plan and council reference numbers

3. Lists non-fixed items

4. Details the settlement

5. Inspection reports

6. Easements and restrictions

7. Cooling off period.

Now, let's get an understanding of these initial steps and what they mean for you.

Points 1, 2 & 3

Points one, two and three are self-explanatory as the terms are somewhat literal in meaning. These points cover off the dimensions and boundary lines, reference numbers perhaps are worthwhile using against a local council search to ascertain future community developments. And lastly, there may be some other features included in the sale such as: furniture or non-fixed appliances and these will be detailed in the contract.

Point 4 - Details the settlement

Point 4 is basically detailing how settlement will take place specifically relating to a time period. This will vary between 30 to 90 days depending and what is agreed at the time of signing the contract. A longer period may provide an advantage to the buyer as it affords more time to finalise the contractual requirements. Conversely it could be viewed as a disadvantage by the vendor particularly if they are hoping for a quicker sale.

Points to consider during the settlement period are:

- There will be a fixed period of time to finalise your finance and also complete inspections.

- Arrange for a final inspection - just to make sure everything is as you remembered.

- Get insurance - You never know what could happen during this period so be careful and always have the appropriate cover. Apart from that once you sign you have what is known as an 'insurable interest' in the property. Lenders will require you as a borrower to arrange an insurance cover or it could cause settlement delays.

Rates, water and perhaps some other charges will need to be rectified between you and the seller. You are responsible for rates and utilities from settlement so make sure you are across this. Also, work on getting your address changed during this period.

Point 5 - Inspection reports

A contract will usually be subject to two main aspects. The first is 'finance' and the second is the 'Building and Pest Inspection', meaning that the contract will only be binding when these conditions are fully satisfied (ie the sale becomes unconditional).

In relation to the inspection (building and pest inspection) reports, it is highly recommended you get one done, as you never really know what lurks beneath the lovely exterior of your potential new home. Inspection costs will generally depend on the size and level of detail required. Remember also that building inspections will also err on the side of caution, purely to indemnify the company conducting the inspection. Bear this in mind during your decision-making process. Also try to be there when the inspection is being carried out so that you can talk directly to the inspector to gain a full understanding about what will be in their report and the caveats. Depending on what's wrong, you may be able to go back to the negotiating table. For example, if prior to signing the contract you didn't know a deck was an illegal extension or that there was an easement running halfway down the side of the block, then you could try to negotiate a lower sale price. Carefully consider each and every aspect or the inspection report, and weigh up your options.

In the ACT generally the seller provides the inspection report. In WA if you wish to carry out inspections, a clause needs to be added to the Offer of Acceptance.

Point 6 - Easements and restrictions

An easement... what's that? An easement is a section of the property which allows someone the right to use the land for a special/ specific purpose, even though they don't own the land. This could be a shared driveway, or buried utilities (power/ phone/ water lines). Easements can cause restrictions and the day the tractor rolls into your backyard to dig up a busted water main (if the yard isn't already flooded) is likely to be a pretty sad one. But easements can also be a great bargaining tool and they do require careful consideration.

Point 7 - Cooling off period

Cooling off periods for NSW/ QLD/ ACT are five days. In the NT, it is four and in VIC, three. In SA, it's two and in WA & TAS, there is no cooling off period. You will need to provide written documentation that you are exiting through the cooling off period before the period ends, in order to cancel the contract. In most cases you will be refunded most of the deposit but in a few States, you may be charged. In NSW it is 0.25% of the purchase price.

Try to not let the real estate agent influence what you insert into contracts. For example, in Victoria, the Real Estate Institute of Victoria has issued a building inspection clause. Therefore, you could look to change the building inspection report so that it allows you to withdraw from the property transaction if the property is "not to the purchaser's satisfaction." As opposed to "major structural defect." Keep in mind that, structural defects are grounds for withdrawing from the contract. However, dodgy wiring or asbestos are not regarded as structural defects and are not reasons to withdraw from the sale. Likewise, make sure fittings and fixtures are listed in the contract as you don't want to find the home stripped bare when you take possession.

So in terms of an ordered process, a private treaty sale will unfold in the following manner:

1. Appoint a conveyancer/ legal representative
2. Exchange contracts
3. Pay the deposit

4. Source insurance cover

5. Cooling off period will be completed

6. Inspection reports completed – land titles are cleared (owned by who they say they are)

7. Finance completed along with a bank valuation

8. Completion of conveyancing (searches complete and the property is unencumbered)

9. Pre-settlement inspection

10. Settlement – pay the remaining funds and take possession and keys.

11. Registration of titles – documents registered with the Titles Office

12. Stamp/ transfer duty payment – required within three months of settlement.

Auction

We went into some detail previously about Auctions but be mindful that the contract you sign at Auction is quite different from a Private Treaty contract. The big differentiator between these two contracts is that auctions are a 'cash' sale in that, upon the fall of the hammer, you are legally bound to exchange contracts and pay a deposit on the day, and there is no cooling off period. Essentially the contract is unconditional on the day. The building and pest inspections will need to be completed **prior** to the auction. If you are interested in the property and intend to bid, get a contract from the agent before the auction and have your legal representative read through it. Seek advice on the terms and have unfavourable conditions deleted or altered. You have an entitlement to change the clauses and if your bid is good enough, they will be flexible. Having the contract checked by your legal rep prior to the auction is imperative in my opinion.

Arrange to have your finance pre-approved as well.

Points to think about:

1. That the property is compliant and that extensions are legal and council-approved.
2. Have inclusions itemized in the contract because if they aren't listed you may not get them.
3. Terms of settlement are as you originally agreed.
4. Deposits can be paid in cash, personal cheque or bank cheque.

In an Auction contract of sale, "bidding conditions" will be outlined by the auctioneer at the beginning of the process. These are put in place so the agent can control the process but ultimately the contract doesn't bind anyone until it is signed. Again though seek professional advice prior to the Auction day.

A property can be bought before the Auction date and it is as simple as making an offer as you would in a private treaty sale. Agents can be a little dismissive of this approach particularly if they are keen to go to Auction so put your offer in writing. Agents can be difficult to deal with in these scenarios as actions are a great opportunity for their self promotion based on the hype an Auction can generate. Also open houses mean meeting more buyers who potentially are sellers and future clients for the real estate agent as well.

The golden rule of thumb is that if it is not in writing or has not been signed by the other party, then the contract is not enforceable.

For more information on Auction rules and regulations, visit the Fair Trading or Consumer Affairs authority in your state or territory.

Off the plan

An 'Off the Plan Contract of Sale' has similarities to a Private Treaty but again there are some big differences. Before signing, speak to a solicitor and make sure some of the following aspects are covered off:

1. A cooling off period
2. Plan disclosures. Normally in larger developments not all aspects will have final government/ council approval. Also, plans will have or cover off interior

145

finishes as well. Before putting your signature anywhere, be absolutely certain you understand the plans and are comfortable with the level of disclosure. Be a devil for the detail in this aspect. As in the Contract of Sale, developers will always retain the right to alter the plans if required so they can finish off the job.

3. Deposit – up to 10% is required and usually it will be held in a trust until settlement. Check who will receive the interest as well. If money is being earned, try to make sure you get it, particularly if the development takes 12 months or more.

4. Inclusions/ warranties – make sure you are protected from overly favourable conditions to the builder and also determine whether you can make your own changes.

5. Finance – make it subject to finance. This is very important as the bank will undertake a valuation on completion of the property. Therefore, you can ensure the finished product's value aligns to what you are going to pay for it.

6. Defects – do a pre-inspection and get any "touch ups" completed before settlement.

7. Completion – timelines for completion will vary and generally the developers will have some flexibility. If the developers cannot complete the property

on time, consider cancelling the contract, as long as you retain the deposit. Again, always seek legal advice.

GETTING OUT OF A CONTRACT

Cooling off period

Cooling off literally means just that because, when the hype dies down and you don't feel right about the purchase, you can pull out.

If you do decide that it's not for you and want out, put it in writing and ideally have it drawn up by your solicitor. Make it official because this will ensure that the initial contract you've entered into is null and void. Be careful if you do reconsider because your deposit will potentially be at stake. Things could get messy if the vendor decides to sue as well. But if it's not for you, like all things in life, just keep walking. The cooling off period will be five days in some states and in others there isn't one at all.

Other contingencies

When you enter into a contract, it is generally done in good faith by both parties. However, there are times when things creep up which can ultimately result in you getting cold feet, beyond the cooling off period. Now there is no "get out of jail free clause" if you do get cold feet. But there are some options which can be leveraged

147

through the contract contingencies. These are usually the appraisal, loan, review of property disclosures, title report etc. For example, if the bank does an appraisal and the valuation is significantly under the purchase price, option one is that you can come to a mutual agreement or you could exit through an appraisal contingency. If the property searches are done and it is found that the boundary lines are ill-defined or an easement runs right through the centre of the house, or if you can't get approved for finance, or the building inspection finds the house is riddled with termites, there are outs for these clauses if they are written into the contract.

Agents will do their best to keep the deal together. Therefore, remember that certain things may allow you to renegotiate or exit the property transaction. If you think that you might get cold feet, don't sign the contract in the first place. There is no sense in putting a lot of time, effort and expense into doing searches, mortgage appraisals, inspections etc if you don't intend to go through with it, and if it all goes wrong, it's your deposit that's at stake. You can generally work through obstacles that arise, however have a good solicitor in case things go sour.

Conveyancer

A conveyancer is a property law specialist who will handle the transfer of the titles.

Conveyancers will lodge the paperwork with the relevant State Department, search the title, and enquire about zoning, rates and outstanding fees associated with existing body corporates. They will liaise between the parties for settlement, ensure special conditions are fulfilled, liaise with the bank, prepare the settlement and attend the settlement on your behalf. They will also field any questions you have, which should include:

1. How much will it cost?
2. How long will it take?
3. What experience do you have in this process?
4. Do you have the support of a solicitor? (eg in case something out of the ordinary arises beyond your expertise)
5. What insurances do you have? (ie to cover you from any negligence on their part. This also ensures they can pay you damages if they are at fault during the process).

You could do your own conveyancing and in some states you can pick up a DIY Conveyancing kit. If you can handle the legal mumbo jumbo, have time and are on a tight budget, it could well be an option. Seeing that it is your first time though, I recommend that you leave it to the professionals.

Timelines

Usually settlement is around six weeks but a short settlement can be as quick as 21 days or less. Settlements can also be a lot longer, depending on what you and the vendor agree to. All in all, settlement times can vary considerably. Below is a rough timeline of events to consider:

Day 1 –

1. Contract agreed and an initial deposit will need to be paid (depending on what state you're in).
2. Engage a mortgage broker/ financial institution to commence seeking finance approval. If you are not pre-approved, commence searching for finance. Visit banks, building societies and speak with brokers ASAP.
3. Engage a conveyancer and organise for building and pest inspection.
4. Organise a cover note through your insurance provider.

Day 7 –

1. Building and pest will be complete.
2. The conveyancer will have liaised regarding contract changes. Once amendments and inspections are complete you will have to provide deposit by cash or use a deposit bond. Once the

150

deposit is paid, the cooling off period is waived and the contract is locked in and binding to both parties.

Day 14 –

1. Contract is binding and you'll know the settlement date and what stamp duty will need to paid.

2. Being a first home buyer you will need to sign the required forms to obtain your buyers grant or stamp duty concession.

3. The conveyancer and bank will liaise, valuation will be complete and contracts exchanged.

4. Transfer of the title deeds will also be lodged so the property can be listed under your own name.

Day 21 –

1. Finance will almost be finalised and cheques are close to getting written.

2. It's time to start arranging for utilities to be connected from settlement, along with redirecting your mail.

3. If you are in a strata arrangement, the body corporate manager will need to be contacted to finalise levies and complete checks.

Day 28 –

1. Finance is approved and the conveyancer will liaise with the parties to ensure titles and finance are in place.

Day 35 –

1. You get the keys, baby! The contract has gone unconditional and is ready for hand over. Finally it's yours. Congratulations!

Costs involved

There are a few little hidden gems when it comes to buying a home. It will feel like you have to keep reaching into your pocket or at least see the bills continue to add up for a whole lot of things that you might not even have considered. To be on the front foot for these expenses (outlined previously on pp. 91).

Upfront and ongoing management of these costs is key to success and key to keeping your head above water. Bills will keep coming, regardless of you wishing they would stop. Budgeting, saving and continuous ongoing management of household expenditure will help ensure you can pay the bills and also maintain a lifestyle that suits your circumstances.

KEY CHAPTER POINTS

1. Contracts are king and there are likely to be three types that you will encounter:

   o Private Treaty Sales: legally binding once both parties sign and ensure the property is not sold to another. The essence of the contract is a checklist that covers off several specific points.

   o Auctions: are a cash sale. A deposit will be required on the day. Building/ pest inspections will be required to be completed prior to auction day. Contracts will also need to be reviewed prior to auction. A property can be brought prior to auction – it just requires the 'right' offer to be submitted.

   o Off the Plan: similar to a Private Treaty but it will include plan disclosures which include the interior finishes. A deposit will need to be paid and will be held in a trust. Warranties will need to be included and will require an aspect to cover off defects for "touch ups" that could be required. Completion timelines require definition and you need to think through your position if the home is not completed on time.

2. Getting out of a contract can be done through a cooling off period. There are

other contingencies in a contract that will also allow you to pull out. The main ones include securing finance; and satisfactory building and pest inspections.

3. Use a conveyancer especially if it is your first property purchase.

4. A lot of costs are involved in the purchase of a property. There can be niggling ones and some you haven't thought of which can really increase your expenses. Be informed and ask everyone upfront about all the costs involved in the purchase.

MISCELLANEOUS ITEMS AND OTHER CONSIDERATIONS

There could be a better title but "Miscellaneous" is probably appropriate. Buying a house is complex, and although we have covered many topics, other things could also be considered. So what are they? How will they affect you? Well, like all things it just depends. Depending on you and your circumstances, some of these options could be realistic or unrealistic. Either way, it is worthwhile having an awareness of a range of other related matters.

ALTERNATIVE OPTIONS:

Buy an investment property

Don't go it alone

Lodgers and flat mates

Individuals living abroad and looking to buy (Foreign Investment Review Board [FIRB])

Buy an investment property

Who said that you need to buy a home before an investment property? Rules, rules... there are no rules. Rent that bad boy out, claim the deductions and gain on capital growth. A clever purchase, a little patience and you could reap the rewards. I did it myself several times. This is a personal favourite of mine and was largely the reason why I was able to buy at such an early age. I benefited from the tax deductions, and the weekly rent cheque was the boost I needed to make this work.

This can be a financially sound option but it won't be suitable for everyone. Professional advice should definitely be sought prior to exercising this option. Be mindful that if you receive the home buyers grant you will have to live in the property. The grant could be sacrificed if you rent out the property straight after purchase. It is a factor that should be factored into your best/ worst case costing scenario.

Rough example of how the numbers could work -

This would be based on an income of $65k, with a purchase price of $550k borrowing 80% of the purchase price:

Income (gross per week)	$1250
Rent (per week)	$400
=	$1650
Income (net)	$980
Rent	$400
=	$1380

EXPENSES

Repayments on $520k (80% of $550k) over 25 years at 5.75% principal and interest loan = $754 per week

$1360 – $754 = $606 per week

There will be additional expenses to account for which include insurance, rates, and water. Potentially the property could sit vacant for a period of time, or maybe a bad lot of tenants will go through the property. All that considered, can you still make ends meet with $606 per week?

Advantage taxation... owning the property as a rental will allow for a number of income deductions. The interest on the loan the expenses mentioned above along with the depreciation will all be factored at tax time. To maximise the benefits, get a quantity surveyor to do a depreciation schedule (costing approx. $1000) and speak to a qualified accountant. Professional advice is an absolute must.

	Credit	Debit (Approx. figures)
Income	$65,000	
Rent	$20,800	
Income tax		$14,000
Interest repayments		$30,000
Rates		$2,000**
Insurance		$1,000**
Utilities and miscellaneous		$5,000**
TOTAL	$85,800	$52,000

** *is a deduction from the tax man. Nice huh? Get the right advice and really crunch the numbers. But an investment property has the potential to really work in your favour.*

Careful consideration needs to be made against rental yields, demand etc. Maybe after a little bit of time you can use the equity built in the property to buy another. Before you know it, you could become a property tycoon.

- Aspects to consider:
- Capital growth
- Demand for rentals in the area
- Maintenance requirements
- Depreciation
- Rates of return
- Income tax implications
- Interest rates
- Expenses.

Similar to purchasing a house to live in, consider aspects like transport/ schools/ proximity to amenities etc. which will be important to tenants. Seek professional advice and above all, aim to get quality tenants who will treat your home the way would.

Tips:

- Look at positive and negative gearing options
- Choose a suitable loan
- Weigh up both principal & interest, and interest-only loans

- Take a long-term approach. This is particularly important because property values will only truly appreciate over time.

Don't go it alone

This doesn't need to be a one-person job. But wow, this is a big consideration because it means if it goes foul, the fallout will be pretty painful. I'm probably being a pessimist with this one but do be careful. If you decide that you'll team up with a good friend, a brother, sister or that special person in your life, make sure there are clear expectations on income and what the long-term plans will be. If you are entering into an arrangement with another, consider what would happen if the other lost their job and had to sit on the bench for some time. What happens if that special person became enemy number one?

Teaming up with someone else is an option to definitely consider and, if done well, it'll allow you to be in that place sooner, and could mean bankable dollars as well. If it goes ugly, well, you will have to deal with the fallout when it happens. If it is a friend or family member, make sure they are "house trained." Set out some ground rules. OK, it might sound drastic but just cover the options beforehand. If it's decided over beers or a bucket of wine, maybe sleep on it. As we all know, sometimes inebriated decisions aren't necessarily the best.

Some practical tips:

- See a solicitor and get some paperwork drawn up. It will act like a condom... it's there for protection. Make a binding agreement on the arrangement you enter into.

- First Home Buyer's Grants: If you are purchasing with one other person, you'll receive only one payment. The grant is payable per property purchase, not per individual.

- If your partner has also owned property before jointly or separately and received the grant, you won't be eligible to receive it.

When you purchase a house with another person, it will be owned under a Joint Tenants or as a Tenant's in Common. Under a Joint Tenants scenario, each owner effectively owns the lot, on the basis that if the other person dies, the other individual will acquire the other half. In Tenants in Common, each person holds their share outright. Therefore, if one dies, the property ownership can be passed onto the next of kin or whoever is outlined in their will. Solicitors will be able to draw up the appropriate paperwork and provide advice on the best options for you and your partner.

Lodgers and flatmates

Don't let the taxman catch you but you could rent out a room with a lodger. It makes sense if you you've bought a new big, bright, shiny house and two bedrooms are going to sit empty. If you do decide to rent out the rooms and bring in some lodgers, it will be considered as income by the ATO unless you have a shared laundry facility or some other shared space – so consult a good tax agent for advice. If you do declare this income, the implications could affect your First Home Buyer's Grant and if you sell the property, you will also be slugged for capital gains tax. Although, a couple of rooms with lodgers and a few hundred extra bucks per week could really come in handy. Ultimately though, the choice is yours. Also, lenders won't take this income into consideration when assessing your ability to service the loan.

Foreign Investment Review Board (FIRB)

For non-Australian citizens abroad and looking to invest in residential property, your purchase will be come under the scrutiny of the Foreign Investment Review Board. Now, there has been a lot of recent publicity that the Board is failing to enforce the rules. Action has been spoken about and high-profile cases have been pursued but it's likely to continue to be discussed by politicians. Being a hot-button issue that is loaded with sensitivities, true change is probably a long time in the making. In the meantime, here are some things to consider if you are a non-Australian citizen:

- property can be purchased in off-the-plan arrangements.

- purchasing establishing homes is not permitted – there are some exceptions.

- Living in Australia on a temporary basis will allow a home to be bought whilst in the country. The property is to be sold within a constricted timeframe.*

*This last point is where the more recent criticism comes from as this often goes unchecked.

For a detailed understanding of the conditions and constraints refer to – www.firb.gov.au

GETTING INTO THAT NEW HOME

Preparing your crib

Moving tips

Renovating

Styling like a star

Managing your ongoing commitments

Preparing your crib

It is a modern world we live in so treat yourself and plug in the power and get going. Be organised and get the utilities organised so that the electricity, gas, internet, cable telly, water and phone are live and ready to go. Also, don't forget to change your postal address.

Tips:

- Power – this needs to be connected on a weekday. Organise this in advance. Go green with alternative energy and remember power accounts can be transferred. If you don't pay your bills, expect to sit in the dark.

- Gas – pretty essential stuff so check it's switched on before moving in. Prepare for it to take up to seven days. Again this is a weekday thing. Check the meter and pay for the gas used, not what the last person used.

- Connect both the gas and power at the same time. Organise to have clear access. Maybe have a look at changing your energy plan to source your cheapest option.

- Foxtel/ Internet etc. Call the professionals in and get it set up.

One of the easiest ways now is to use a connection provider. It's quick, simple and saves you the rushing around. It's normally free as well. They can also connect the lot on your behalf, so all systems are go!

Moving tips

1. Get help and try roping in as many friends and family as you can handle for the day. The true tip is providing beers and a BBQ at the end as a way of saying "thank you"

2. De-clutter – moving is a great time to throw things out that you haven't used for a long time. It always feels better when you are lighter. Even better is to offload some of the items for cash through Gumtree or eBay.

3. Get the Internet connected. Sort out your plan and have it up and running. This saves using your phone data in the meantime.

4. Boxes – man, these things can get expensive. Second hand boxes are like gold. Put up an advert on Gumtree and, you never know, someone might be giving them away for free. Label your boxes clearly with their contents – this makes it so much easier deciding which box goes where.

5. Packing – use socks for glasses or other breakables and t-shirts for plates and

crockery, saves on bubble wrap. Popping the bubbles is a lot of fun though. And use glad wrap on open toiletries to prevent spills.

6. Stock up – fill up the trolley, you've got plenty of cupboards now so fill them up. When you first move in and start nesting, chances are you won't want to leave for a while.

7. Get insurance on the hire truck. Forgetting the height and tearing off the gutter when you are backing into the driveway will hurt the truck, the house and your back pocket in a big way!

8. If you're using removalists, ask about additional charges, what hourly rates will actually cover and make sure you read all the terms and conditions. You do have rights to the services you have acquired but don't get caught out with loopholes.

9. Use soap to fill up nail holes, use a bond cleaner and hand the keys back on time. Aim to get every cent of your bond back.

Renovating

It is only natural to want to spruce up your crib. Once you move in, you'll most definitely have a few new ideas on what you'd like to change to ensure that it is looking its best. So how much should you spend? What are the pros and cons? What should you renovate? Additional bedrooms? New deck? New bathroom? How about the kitchen? How long will it take? Here's where you need to keep a firm grip on your budget: furniture and soft furnishings cost good money, and the size of the house or apartment will make a difference to the costs understandably.

Buying a house and then stamping your personality on it is challenging for anyone but it's also really rewarding. There's nothing like a bit of hard yakka, and then standing back with a cold beer and a smile to admire all your handy work.

If you've bought an apartment, it will generally be subject to special considerations. These considerations will apply to noise, fire, privacy, common areas, body corporate regulations and the list goes on. Normally a body corporate will be considered to own everything under the paint and carpet. You normally will have control over everything else. Anything considered "common" will be a no-go zone. Generally it's not worth challenging either because the juice won't be worth the squeeze. Whenever possible, check the guidelines and if you are in doubt, check with the local council.

Getting the necessary approvals in place will be needed if you start tackling anything structural. Extensions will require planning approval – that's a necessity.

The big-ticket items will be:

- Bathroom
- Kitchen
- Extensions.

The options are only limited to your budget. Get quotes, use only qualified builders and do what you can yourself. What could go wrong? Providing an overview of all the aspects for consideration would probably require a whole new book, but go with your style and budget, and do not over-capitalise. Remember: it's your first home, and doesn't necessarily need to be the last. But if it is, knock yourself out but try not to over-capitalise.

Away from the big ticket items, a new paint job, carpets/ flooring and new cabinets can be cost-effective ways of making a big difference to the look and feel of the place. However, you also have to think about the boring but necessary jobs:

- Repairs, maintenance and rectifications. A leaking roof can have disastrous effects.

- Replacing the hot water system will be a better option than choosing a new flat screen (barely just though). This may not initially sound quite right but it will be worth its weight in gold on a cold winter's morning.

Design/ styling on a budget

Don't buy what you are told to buy. Buy something that you know you'll enjoy. If the pool table takes up the whole room, well, who cares? It is your place so go for it! Alternatively, if contemporary chic is your thing, go for that instead. Speaking to interior decorators, they will have a few other tips to provide including:

1. Style like a star – buy something that speaks volumes. One feature piece that you can build a room around. This is the key. Give your furniture some breathing room to prevent a cluttered look.

2. Dark paint colours actually make a small room look bigger. However, don't let it affect your lighting because that's all important too. Ambient light for mood and direct light for reading. Layer the lighting, darling. Layer the lighting.

3. Pimp out the bedroom. Nothing better than a good night sleep, is there? Nice sheets, luxury pillows and an extra big bed will make you love life much more after a good night's sleep. Equally important is a good couch. The couch is the perfect place to drop your anchor on a lazy afternoon, so make it a good investment.

4. It might be a man's things but all work and no play is never really that much fun. So if you're lucky enough to have some spare change after buying all of the above, invest the rest in the box. A good quality, high definition TV with surround sound will definitely be used over and over. Plus, Game of Thrones will be so much better.

5. Try second-hand shopping. Not only is it a bit of fun, it's more interesting compared to some of the sterile environments of the big furniture stores. It's a great chance to jag some bargains and it's an equally good chance to cash in some of your old gear as well.

6. Be bold. Creativity and a unique individualism make it all that more fun.

Everyone has got his or her own tastes and, once you step into your new HOME, I'm sure some shopping will follow. Go have some fun with it.

Managing costs and ongoing commitments

This raises another interesting point... what happens if you have difficulty making payments. The hot water system dies, the car claps out, the boss gives you the flick and you find out a new bubba is on the way? Wow, talk about feeling stressed! Interest rates may also rise and other bills continue to come in. It may sound a bit drastic and, hopefully, it won't all happen at the one time but, trust me, there will be times that you'll find yourself on struggle street. The hot tip here is not to run, duck and hide but to address it as quickly as you can, in fact, the moment you realise that things are getting out of control.

Firstly, call your credit providers and let them know your current situation to discuss what options are available. When assessing your options, credit providers could be in a position to help (eg arrange a financial variation to the contract) and make sure if there is an alternative repayment plan that you can still afford to make those payments. Keep the payments up, no matter what - or else things will just start getting harder. This is also the time to reassess that budget and really cut it to the bones. Seek a financial counsellor. Determine if there is anything you can sell, refinance or consolidate. If you really have over-committed, you may have to sell and recoup your losses. This is a really unfortunate outcome but it remains a better option than the house being repossessed by the bank.

Note: Don't think that borrowing more will get you out of trouble. This will only be a short-term fix and it will come back to bite you.

This is a really ugly position to find yourself in, as well as incredibly stressful, emotionally draining and just plain eeky. Such as scenario really hits home about the importance of not over-committing to begin with. Also, allow for contingencies and over-estimate costs at the start of your journey so always build in some 'fat' when estimating your costs... all costs!

KEY CHAPTER POINTS

1. Buying an investment property is an alternative consideration that people are pursuing as a way of getting into the property market. The benefit is the rent received and deductions from a taxation perspective which could be enough for you to afford our own home very soon. Different expenses will be encountered and professional advice should be sought.

2. Buying with another individual will mean that you enter into a Joint Tenants or a Tenant's in Common arrangement. Under a Joint Tenants arrangement, each owner effectively owns the lot whereas Tenants in Common means that each person own their share outright. The net effect is the difference on how property ownership will transition should you die.

3. Having someone rent a room could be helpful to the household budget's bottom line. Income that is declared will be taxable and should you sell the property, this income declared would also mean that the property will be exposed to capital gains.

4. When moving, get help, declutter, use innovative ways to pack, get insurance and leave the house spick and span to get your bond back.

5. Renovating options are endless and are only limited by your budget. Do what work you can, enjoy (wherever possible) the stress, and concentrate on the end result because it will be well worthwhile once the hard work is completed.

6. When pimping out your pad, style like a star. Lighting is key and, if you can, spoil yourself with a high-end purchase or two to help you feel that the house really has become your castle.

7. Costs are ongoing and they become similar to annoying friends that you hope would contact you less. But they continue to turn up and happily sit quietly in your letterbox. Ongoing management of mortgage costs, recurring bills and life's lemons means that things can become difficult to manage. If this does become reality, don't hide behind it, speak with your creditors and work out alternative arrangements wherever possible.

THE JARGON GLOSSARY

- Application fee – a charge the bank/ institution applies for the privilege of considering a loan application. Paid upfront and not refundable (generally).
- Auctions – form of selling which creates competition and upon the fall of the hammer, it will be a cash sale. Forces the hand of the buyer to commit.
- Basic variable loan – an interest rate that fluctuates and is benchmarked.
- Body corporate – also known as the 'owner's co-op' is legislation applying to a block that has multiple dwellings. The 'co-op' basically is responsible for the control, maintenance and management of the common area. Generally everything under the paint and carpet is considered to be owned by the 'body corporate'.
- Break costs – charges applied when you're wrapped up in a fixed loan and you pay it off early or before the agreed term.
- Budget – it's a personal financial plan outlining the money coming in and going out.
- Capital gains – these are good ones. It's the profit you take after a higher sale than the original purchase price.
- Contract of Sale – legally binding contract that allows the property transaction to take place between the separate parties.
- Construction loan – this is where the funds of the loan are disbursed when stages are completed or at agreed time intervals.

- Conveyancer – this is what happens when the property title is transferred from one to another.
- Comparison rate – helps the borrower work out what the true cost of the loan actually is. Includes the actual rate and all fees and charges in a single figure.
- Cooling off – after the contract is signed, there is a period of time where the contract can be cancelled without penalty.
- Credit – money that is coming into your bank account like your wage.
- Daily interest – the interest on a loan is calculated every day for the life of the loan.
- Debit – money that is going out of your bank account like any general expense.
- Defects – something that just isn't quite right… an imperfection.
- Deposit – what you slog out by not eating out, quitting drinking and your social life ending ☺
- Depreciation – the wear, tear and use of something of value (an asset) will reduce in value overtime.
- Deposit bonds – an alternative to a cash deposit. Held in a trust until settlement when the remainder of the purchase price is paid.
- Disclosures – something 'unknown' or kept 'hush hush' is now out there and known.
- Equity – equity mate! Much like capital gains we like this one too. This is the difference in property value to the outstanding loan value.
- Easement – the right to cross or access your block for a special purpose.

- First Home Buyers Grant – a little cash offering from the government to give you a helping hand for your first buy. A one-off payment.

- Fixed rate loans – the rate does not move for an agreed period of time. Big benefit is that you'll know what your commitment is for that period. Con is that is offers little flexibility to other products.

- Goals – the aim of the end result that you are looking to achieve.

- Guarantor – if you ask your Mum and Dad nicely they may act as one. Basically the other person puts up their assets to guarantee the loan. Builds assurance for the lender that they can recoup their money should a default occur.

- Holding deposit – putting down some upfront cash as a show of good faith that you'll follow through with the transaction.

- Income statement – a summary of how much coinage you produce. Proof as well that you actually earn it.

- Joint tenants – in short, if one dies the other party picks up their share as opposed to the ownership being passed to a next of kin.

- Landlord – someone who rents out a house, flat, land, building etc.

- Lender mortgage insurance – borrowing more than 80%? Expect to get hit with this. It's a security cost for insurance to protect the lender (bank) as you are considered a high risk.

- Liabilities – generally it means money that is owed and you have a responsibility to repay it.

- Line of credit – where you strike a deal with the bank that allows you to draw on the line of credit you have, as long as you don't exceed the agreed terms.

- Low Doc Loans – bank will consider the loan application with reduced document or verified statements

- Loan to value ration – divide the property value by the amount of the loan. Really it is the value of what you are borrowing.

- Mortgage – the bank lends you the money, slaps on some fees and charges interest on top of the principal sum that you repay over the next 25 – 30 years.

- Mortgagor – the borrower in the mortgage i.e. you.

- Mortgagee – the lender i.e. the bank.

- Mortgage broker – renders services to procure the loan on your behalf.

- Mortgage protection insurance – life insurance policy designed to pay off the mortgage if you become "brown bread' (dead) while you're paying off the home.

- Non-conforming loans – fails to stick to the banks guidelines.

- Offset account – like a day-to-day account that is linked to the home loan. The credit of the account then offsets the daily interest against the reminding balance.

- Ombudsmen – a complaints investigator.

- Principal – the sum of money owed.

178

- Principal and interest – money owed with interest on top.
- Rates – the levy charged by your local council for land tax and costs associated with services provided.
- Rates of return – how an asset has tracked over a period of time in terms of financial return.
- Redraw facility – similar to offset account (refer to the above).
- Security – assets used to cover the loan liabilities.
- Standard variable rate – most common loan rate after the honeymoon discount rate finishes.
- Stamp Duty – levied by the states when you purchase property. Will likely be your single largest expense after the purchase itself.
- Stick-to-itiveness – not giving up and sticking to the plan.
- Tenants in common – this is where one or more owns separate portions of the property. If one person dies, the property passes to the descendants not the other owners.
- Unencumbered – no liabilities or restrictions on the property.
- Valuation – an estimated worth. Typically done prior to the loan approval.
- Vendor – the person offering the property sale.

www.ingramcontent.com/pod-product-compliance
Lightning Source LLC
Chambersburg PA
CBHW060026210326
41520CB00009B/1015